The

Prince

&

The

Pauper

Revised Edition

Agu Jaachynma N.E.

The Prince & The Pauper, Revised Edition
Copyright © 2015 Agu Jaachynma N.E.
Email: nkeafam@yahoo.com

First Published by Enaz Publications 2008

Revised Edition by Chiysonovelty International, 2015

ISBN: 9785317609

ISBN-13: 978-9785317602

Chiysonovelty International
Plot 8 Evule Avenue
Aba,
Nigeria
Email: chiyson@minister.com
Phone: 234-818-118-3131

Printed in the United States of America

Scripture quotations are taken from the King James Version and the New King James Version of the Bible.

The views expressed in this work are solely those of the author and do not necessarily reflect the views of the Publisher, and the Publisher hereby disclaims any responsibility for them.

DEDICATION

To my Husband: *Dr. Aham* and my Sons: *King & Edwald*...

It's Liquid Love All the Way!

And We Say…

"*THE PRINCE AND THE PAUPER*" is a thought promoting masterpiece from the stable of *Jaachy* an amiable Christian author. The book is a pointer to those seeking direction. It is an uplifting, spirit- filled masterpiece for the whole family. Strongly recommended for those desiring a change in their lives… no matter the level of life you are living now, there is always a HIGHER LIFE.

Dr. Agu Ahamefula (*Author's spouse*)

Dept. of Obstetrics & Gynaecology, ABSUTH, Abia State, Nigeria.

Jaachy in "*The PRINCE AND THE PAUPER*" displayed a prolific prowess in writing. A new dimension in Christian literature set for both Christians and Non-Christians who desire a personal encounter with the PRINCE. The book is a thriller of our time…

Pastor Enoch Nwachara

UJAT Construction Company, Abuja, Nigeria.

Beautiful, Wonderful and Powerful. I wish a copy of this concise and highly readable work had been available when I wrote my best-selling knowledge book: "*The Sagacity of Sage.*"

Anyaele, Sam Chiyson (*Engineer / Businessman / Author*)

2

The *"PRINCE AND THE PAUPER"* is a life transforming information wrapped and delivered in a simple and understandable language. The Author took time and carefully unraveled the reason for failure, lack, criminality, addiction and all other vices we see in the world today.

An undeniable truth is that *"there are no God-made failures."* The decision *"to be"* and *"to have"* is totally human. You are the CEO of your life, so cease from making peace, make policies. I strongly recommend this book to youths in our primary and secondary schools as well as the tertiary Institutions.

It is also a MUST read for parents who wish to chart a good course for themselves and their wards. For those who desire to retrace their steps and paths, it is a companion, for those whose lives are hanging on an unbalanced balance, it is a pivot, for those who have given up hope in life, it's a stimulant and for some whose mindsets are wrongly programmed, it is reprogramming software.

Chima Azubike

Financial Analyst.

CONTENT

FOREWORD

LIFE is the sum total of the choices we make each day. No matter how long we live here on earth, the length is still too short when compared to eternity. This is why it is important we do not play games or gamble with our lives here on earth.

Though your beginning was small, yet you can expressively enhance your end, so says the scriptures. You can walk out on your past if you choose to. You can leave the failures and mediocrity of yesterday behind and move on to a glorious future already prepared for you.

The fact still remains that while some choose to stick to their past glories, failures, achievements et al others are smarter and so choose to meet the PRINCE who changes the lives and destinies of as many as are willing to come to Him in faith. Faith is Now! You are a chosen generation; you are a royal priesthood. You are of the royal class so royalty is in your blood…you should not be a pauper for the PRINCE became poor for you to be rich.

Read this book with an open heart and mind. Discover the package the PRINCE has for you and importantly, learn how to walk out on your past and move into your glorious future. Yes, into your Beautiful Life.

Rev. Sam Iheanacho

Grace of God Mission Int'l.

His Glory Parish, Enugu State, Nigeria.

ACKNOWLEDGMENTS

I thank the Almighty God who gave me the grace and ability to birth this book. Thank You my Lord Jesus Christ for standing by me through it all. I love and exalt the Holy Spirit for the inspiration He gave me.

To my beloved Mum- **Mrs M.N. Iheanacho,** who trained us in the path of truth: thanks a million, Maama…You are the Best! Thank you **Phidel, Clara, Stella & Enkay** my lovely elder sisters for leading me aright via godly examples and standards, I love you all.

I appreciate my younger brother - **Rev. Sam** for your implicit faith in me, much love kid brother! …and **Ify,** you are too much…Thanks too!

My Bunch of Cutie Pies…**Debby, Sammie, Favour, Josh, Sam (Jnr) & Chidera**…you are too sweet.

I deeply appreciate my husband - **Dr Ahamefula Agu,** your love is so true, so real and so pure. You mean the world to me and I value you all ways and always. I love you much more.

My heartfelt affection is for you – **King** and **Edwald** – my Gorgeous Heritages; you are the BEST, you are here for SIGNS and WONDERS…Mummy is so proud of you!

To my Pastors - *Pastor Archie, Pastor Ngy & Pastor Callistus Inwalome,* thank you for being what God wants you to be in my life at different towns and time. Thank you also for loving the body of Christ immensely! God bless you all.

My friends - *Adayuk, Ogey, Esther, Oluchi, Ifeanyi, Sheri, Doris* and others too numerous to mention, for your exciting e-mails, text messages, phone calls, love and friendship, I am grateful and excited knowing you all.

Sister **Esther**, for painstakingly typing the first manuscript, I say thank you.

Pastor **Enoch Nwachara**, for editing and re-typing the first edition, much thanks!

Engr. **Chiyson Sam Anyaele**....you are an encouragement, thank you so much.

To *Mr. & Mrs Otuechere, Dr. & Barr. Anele Agu, Chief (Barr) & Lolo C. Ekwomadu, Mr. & Mrs G. C Nwichi, Mr. B. A. Nwokocha, Dr & Mrs A. Iheanacho, Dr. & Mrs Ezirim, Dr & Mrs Ndukwe O.O*...THANKS.

Finally, to those whom I met when I was down, come up, there is a lot of space up here.

God bless you all.

"Your qualification and position has nothing to do with it, If you haven`t had an encounter with the Prince of Peace, you are a pauper."
                              - Agu Jaachynma N.E.

Introduction

The Prince and the Pauper

A prince is a leading light, a leading figure and a big shot, highly regarded and honoured. When a prince is born, everyone rejoices and nations celebrate because an outstanding personality is born.

The Bible says in the book of **Isaiah 9:6**, *"For unto us a child is born, unto us a son is given, and the government shall be upon his shoulder, and his name shall be called Wonderful, Counsellor, The Mighty God, The Everlasting Father, The PRINCE OF PEACE..."*

Jesus Christ is the Prince; He is the Gift of a Son to us. His birth brought the higher life to us and empowered us to run the affairs of this world successively. From the verse above, we saw the Prince is associated with names like Amazing Counselor, Strong God, Eternal Father and Prince of Wholeness. He knows who He is and manifests His eternal glory unprecedentedly.

On the other hand, the pauper is a down-and-out person, a poor fellow whose mentality is very shallow.

He is a person who thinks he has no grip on life and who feels his years on earth are wasted.

It doesn`t matter how one tries to change the pauper, he is always full of excuses. He has his own expressions, which do not measure up to the higher life. He is always asking for hand-me-downs.

He sees himself as someone always in need and complains ceaselessly about his needs. His mindset and daily confession goes thus: *"But I am POOR and NEEDY, make haste unto me O God: thou art my help and my deliverer, O Lord, make no tarrying!"* (**Psalm 70:5**)

The good news is the pauper`s life can be transformed by his refusal to remain comfortable in the low-life. His mind can be renewed by fixing his attention on God who will transform him from the inside out.

The pauper can give his life to God and allow Him bring out the best in him. The pauper can find rest and receive God's special kind of knowledge to live the Princely life.

Jesus Christ calls out in the book of **Matthew 11:28-30,** *"Come unto me all ye that Labour and are heavy laden* *and I will give you rest. Take my yoke upon you and learn of me, for I am meek and lowly in heart, and ye shall find rest unto your souls. For my yoke is easy, my burden is light."*

The state of any pauper is traumatic; it's painful, hurting, disappointing, humiliating and embarrassing. Why would you want to dwell in a place not meant for you by destiny? This call to change requires urgent attention. Don't postpone your response for today is the tomorrow you talked about yesterday.

Changing your life for the better is your responsibility; you can enhance your status and have a great life like the Prince. Yes, all you need do is change your orientation and have faith in the Lord Jesus Christ; He can make you whole, change your status, and add value to your destiny.

Hear what Apostle Paul told the Jailer in the Book of **Acts 16:31**, *"Believe on the Lord Jesus Christ, and thou shall be saved, and thy house"*.

It is my message to you as well! Receive this message of salvation today!

John 5:24 reaffirms this *"Verily, verily I say unto you, he who hears my word and BELIEVES in Him who sent me,* *has eternal life and shall not come into Judgment but has passed from death to life."*

You can recreate your world with the Word of the Creator in your mouth. Living the princely life requires you learn how to think, reason and act like the prince. Your world of poverty can be recreated to one of affluence just by speaking the prince's language.

The Psalmist said in **Psalms 119: 105,116** *"Your word is a lamp unto my feet and a light unto my path. Uphold me according to your word that I may live and do not let me be ashamed of my hope."*

This book came as a *tool* to help you work with the spoken Word of the King. Any pauper that heeds the call of the Prince will drop off all *"Pauperic"* garments and weight.

Dress up with the robe of righteousness; lay down those burdens and travel light

You cannot dress in those pitiable attires and dine on the Master's table. Your outfit must change same with your mindset and reasoning. The Blind Bartimaeus caught this secret, by the time the Master, the Prince of Peace called out to him; he put away his beggarly garment and rushed to the Saviour.

Make up your mind to accept the invitation of the Prince of Peace today. Allowing the Prince of Peace in, gives you the ability to stop thinking and start reasoning.

Reasoning is what you do beyond the depth of your normal thinking; it is the ability to use your sixth sense to find solutions and produce striking results. Your reasoning depends on a set of beliefs, it is a special way of thinking and it determines your behaviour as well as your looks.

Your mindset plays a very important role in this business. The programming of your human mind to act in a certain way is very significant. What you believe is what you become; answering the call endows you with the ability to live the princely life.

Philippians 4:8-9 (MSG) says *"Summing it all up, friends, I'd say you'll do best by filling your minds and meditating on things true, noble, reputable, authentic, compelling, gracious—the best, not the worst; the beautiful, not the ugly; things to praise, not things to curse. Put into practice what you learned from me, what you heard and saw and* *realized. Do that, and God, who makes everything work together, will work you into his most excellent harmonies."*

Working your way into God's most excellent harmonies is patterning your life in accordance with the Word of God so as to enjoy the princely life. In this life, you only display virtues and grace.

Where you are at the moment is the product of the choices you made in the past. The way you set your mind to work determines your position and choices in life.

The Prince lives the excellent life, he knows he has an extraordinary driving force, which determines the way he positions himself and how he makes his choices. He knows his life is not ordinary so he charts the course of his life with the Word.

Word triggered reasoning yields result. Creative thinking encompassed by the Word of God infuses into you the divine ability to turn the seemingly ugly situation around.

When you begin to reason with the Lord, your attitude to life's issues will change. Your actions are the products of your thoughts and your thought is influenced by your source of inspiration and ideas.

Make God's "thinkings" and words the source of your ideas and so you can experience unhindered access to the great life.

God reasons differently from man and He desires for man to come up to His level of reasoning that is why He made man in His own Image and after His likeness.

Reasoning like God places you in His class. Learn to leverage on God's word, it is the only tool for lasting change. Studying and meditation on God's Word enables you to capture God's thoughts and His ways of doing things.

You are a prince with the mind of Christ however not to many people reason like Christ or make His words their inspiration.

"...because as he is, so are we in this world" (1 John 4: 17). Though you see yourself as human, yet you have the nature of Christ. With your spirit, you can attract advancement, wealth and distinction.

Your spirit is the real you, your spirit became born again during your salvation experience and your spirit is made in God's image. Man is a tripartite being, he has *three* components comprising of the Spirit, the Soul and the Body.

As we have earlier mentioned the spirit is the real you, the soul is your seat of emotions, your will-power and your mind. Your body is the physical you, it acts like the house to your spirit and soul. Without your body, your spirit cannot function in this physical world.

Physically speaking, man has the *appearance, speech* and *behaviour.* Your appearance is your looks, the way you dress. Your attire reflects your sense of value and taste. Naturally, people will always address you based on the way you dress.

Your speech either makes or mars you, "*Death and life are in the power of the tongue: and they that love it shall eat the fruit thereof.*" **(Proverbs 18:21)**

You are what you speak so you are advised to speak right always. You should say what you mean and mean what you say.

Your behaviour is the sum total of your action and reaction to issues and people around you. It tells who you are, who dwells in you, whether you are normal or abnormal.

It matters how your spirit, soul and body are conditioned. Where you place yourself and whom you choose to become is the unique manifestation of the workings of your spirit, soul and body.

The aim of this book is to help you understand who you really are and what you have in Christ. Christ is not just a Personality, He is also a Place; when in Him, you experience the beautiful life. He is not against you and He is not angry with you either.

The Prince of God is here to understand you, to listen to all your tales of woe, to straighten your rugged path and make a winner out of you. There is a remarkable difference between a Prince and a pauper.

The Prince has the Spirit of the Lord and so knows what God has in stock for him but the pauper does not know what the future holds for him, he struggles for everything; he lies, cheats and does all sorts of evil vices to *"belong or become."* Ignoring the Prince`s invitation of *"follow me and I will make you."*

Moving from the *"pauperic"* position to the Princely position is a decision worth taking. It doesn't take much to move higher because the provisions have been made, the foundation is already laid, *"For other foundation can no man lay than that is laid, which is Jesus Christ."* (**1ˢᵗ Corinthians 3:11**)

Jesus Christ is the foundation! All you need do is to build on this foundation and build accordingly.

This book is Holy-Sprit inspired, it is aimed at giving you day-to-day details of how to live your life, how to move from the *"pauperic"* stage to the Princely stage, how to experience what you expect, and get your dreams and desires fulfilled.

Do you want to make a change? Are you tired of living like a destitute? Do you want to rise and shine? Do you want to flourish? This book will help you achieve them all. It will aid your advancement in destiny.

You are programmed for the top; your choice and decision is crucial in shaping your destiny. Do you desire this change? Then let's move at God's pace.

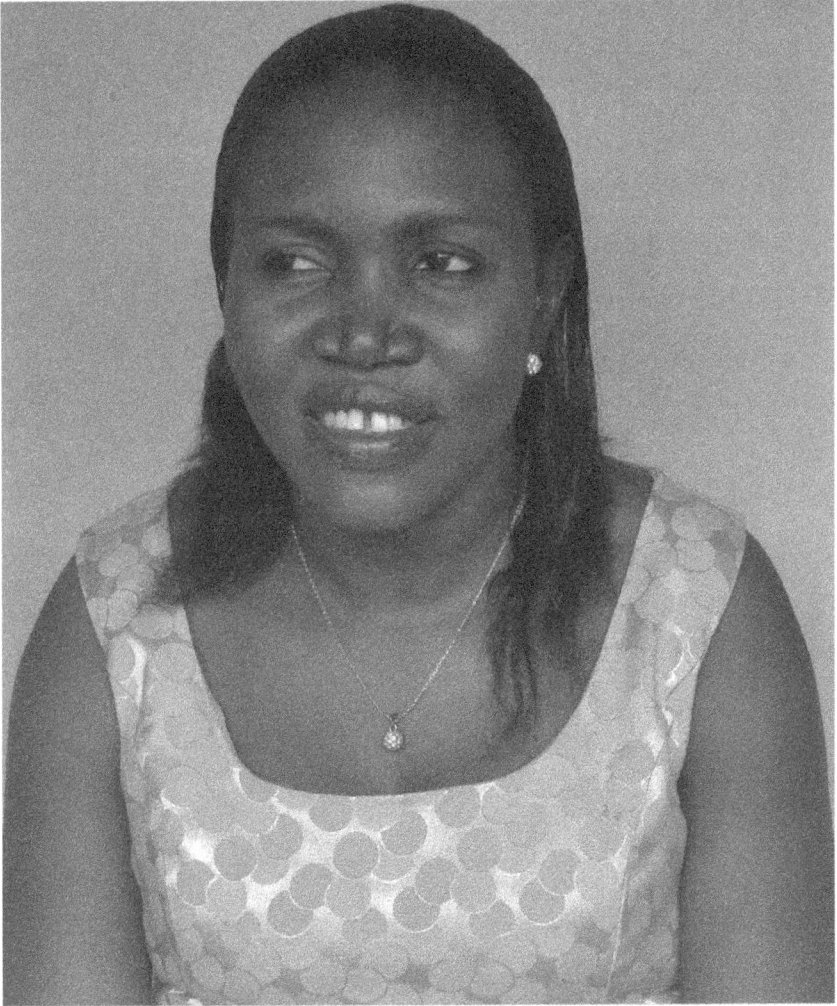

"Your world of poverty can be recreated to one of affluence just by speaking the Princely language."
- Agu Jaachynma N.E.

Chapter One

Who is This Pauper?

The Oxford Advance Learner's Dictionary defined *"Pauper"* as a very poor person. Now, here is the million-dollar question: *who is a poor person?* A person is said to be poor when he doesn't have adequate means or resources to meet his demands or needs.

A poor person lacks virtually all life's goodies and comfort; a poor person is always in want. There are different classes of poverty such as mental, spiritual, physical, financial, emotional and social poverty.

Matthew 5:3, *"Blessed are the poor in spirit for theirs is the Kingdom of heaven."*

Being *"poor in spirit"* is not the same as being *spiritually poor*. Someone who is poor in spirit is humble, gentle, meek, God-fearing and kind. He exhibits the fruits of the Holy Spirit but one who is *"Spiritually poor"* lacks everything that pertains to life and godliness.

He is virtually empty of the favours and flavours of God. Great possession of material things amount to nothing when there is less of God and more of self.

A spiritually poor fellow lacks the grace of our Lord Jesus Christ, the love of God and the relationship with the Holy Spirit. He lacks divine knowledge, Godly ideas and can hardly see beyond his nose. The pitiable aspect of it is he lacks the *know-how* of seeking the knowledge he lacks. This divine knowledge delivers to people their estates in God. Anyone lacking in this knowledge is a prey to destruction for this knowledge is a defence.

Hosea 4:6, *"My People are destroyed for lack of knowledge because thou hast rejected knowledge, I will also reject thee, that thou shall be no priest to me: seeing thou hast forgotten the law of thy God, I will also forget thy children."*

Knowledge is very vital in life's transformation and transition. I believe *"You are known for what you know."*

The pauper doesn't know what's right or true; he has no knowledge of God's plans and purpose for his life. He is self-conscious and not God-conscious. Spiritual things are impossible for him to decipher.

For instance, he does not understand that a *"breakdown"* can turn to a *"breakthrough."* An intimate relationship with God sounds strange to him because he sees himself as minute and insignificant.

He is yet to come to terms with the price Christ paid

for the souls of men. He thinks his good deeds will take him to heaven.

He ignores the Spirit of truth sent to be his Friend, Teacher, Counsellor, Confidant and Comforter. He goes about with his cloak of self-righteousness and faith in man rather than God.

The pauper may be wealthy with material things, he may be educated with several degrees, with lots of titles to his name; he may be an elder in a church or a member of different cults. His position in the church and society doesn`t count, he is poor indeed if he doesn`t have the fear of God. The pauper is a spiritually poor person. He lacks God`s favor and the knowledge of God`s Word.

I was told this story of a man whom I will refer to as John. John went to his father one morning and said *"Dad, I want to let you know what I will prefer as a gift from you during my birthday which equally coincides with my graduation from college."*

The father agreed and asked him to go ahead. John went on to describe a particular sports car he saw at the Garage of well-known car dealer. After all said and done, he left his father, excited that he will have the keys to the car soonest.

On the morning of his birthday and graduation, his father invited John to his room, congratulated and counseled him then gave him a gift wrapped with a brightly coloured wrap sheet. John's countenance fell; this was not what he expected from his father. No, not after he made a passionate request to his Dad.

However, out of curiosity, he tore the sheets open and discovered a beautiful leather backed King James Version of the Bible. John was furious; enraged, he flung the gift away to his father.

What nonsense! How could Dad be this callous? John stormed out of the room picked his few belongings and left the house.

He was away, struggling, sweating and trying all on his own to make ends meet so he could eventually go for that car but all was to no avail.

Eventually, he got a message that his Dad was on his deathbed; he decided to pay him a final visit. He travelled home to see his dying *wicked* father. As soon as he set his foot into the father's room, the man breathed his last.

Beside the man's bed was a stool and on it was the same gift John rejected several years back. Still untouched with half of the wrap sheet torn, John picked it up and carefully removed the wrap sheet, then he noticed something like a page marker in between the pages of the Bible.

He opened to the page and saw a car key with a tag *"fully paid for"* marked on it. He turned the other side of the tag and read to his amazement the address of the car dealer and the description of the car he requested for few days to his graduation ceremony.

He looked closely at the page of the Bible where the key was inserted and saw: **Mathew 7:7-11** with verse 11 carefully marked by his father, *"…If ye then being evil know how to give good gifts unto your children, how much more shall your father which is in Heaven give good things to them that ask him?"*

John wept sorely. All these years he has been a car owner without knowing it, he has left a beautiful car parked at a place that it was not needed, he has remained a poor man whereas he was wealthy, and he has even been ungrateful to a father who has been so kind to grant him his wish!

John remained a pauper even when provisions were made for his up-liftment. John remained with the downtrodden, trekking miles, sweating to make ends meet because he was ignorant of what already belonged to him. John was even struggling to get some money to go for that car not knowing the car was already his.

John was an example of a spiritually poor fellow! He was unappreciative and lacked knowledge. He depicted the life of several paupers today who treat as unimportant all of God`s provision for them. They prefer it the tough way; their slogan usually is *"good things don't come easy."*

How wrong they are! The air we breathe is good, isn't it? How much do we pay, queue or struggle to acquire it? The rains and sunshine are beautiful and essential to man, animals and plants. What do we do to have them? Absolutely nothing!

How much did we pay Christ to die in our stead? Did we pay for Christ's sacrificial death on the cross? No! Just like John`s father did, Christ fully paid the price for the beautiful life. Ours is to take pleasure in and from this gift!

The pauper now has a right to the higher life; he can live free from sin and curses, he can enjoy eternal life now. The power of death is broken; Jesus lives forever! We are saved…yes; we are the fruits of redemption! Praise God!

There is hope for the pauper, there is bread for the hungry, there is grace to help in times of need. The captives have been set free and the captivity is taken captive. Don't allow ignorance to further enslave your destiny.

God`s plan is for you to have and enjoy a colourful destiny, He already made provisions for a delightful destiny for you in Christ Jesus. Hence His call to you in **Isaiah 1:18-19:** *"Come now, and let us reason together, Saith the Lord: though your sins be as dark as scarlet, they shall be as white as snow, though they be as red as crimson, they shall be as wool. If ye be willing and obedient, ye shall eat the good of the land."*

Don`t desire it the hard and tough way; change your mindset from *"the-sweat-to-sweet"* pattern to *"sweet-sweet"* all the way! Your position and placement in life is already settled.

You need to be properly positioned so as to have a

clearer view of your mission and how to achieve your vision in life. Salvation helps you do this; God already settled the placement issue for all humanity.

It doesn't matter where man placed you, what matters is your divine placement in life; your being properly positioned in Christ. If you are still unsure of where your foot is placed then you are a pauper, you are wretched and pitiable.

Wealth without Christ leads to foolishness and destruction, life without Christ is always full of crises.

Don't be deceived, take a stand now and move from darkness into light. Choose to live in God's palace instead of in holes and dungeon. Make up your mind and be adorned with princely regalia rather than the beggarly garments. Position yourself rightly in Christ today.

Deuteronomy 30:19, *"I call heaven and earth to record this day against you, that I have set before you life and death, blessing and cursing: Therefore choose life that both thou and thy seed may live."*

God wants you to choose life over death, choose to be a prince rather than be a pauper. The Bible tells us of leading lights; people who stood out and took their proper places in God.

Joshua was one of them, he pursued his vision with zeal and accomplished his mission because he found his place in God. How did he do it? He refused to go with the majority who were spiritually poor and blind. He didn`t give the daily situations the ability to becloud his sense of reasoning and value.

Amongst the spies sent by Moses to check out the land of Canaan, Joshua and Caleb brought back good report concerning the land while the other spies whom I describe as paupers gave the people of Isreal negative reports about the land.

Two groups of people stood at the same spot, had a view of a place but came up with different reports because of their different placements in life.

Joshua and Caleb understood God has placed them and no man can move them. They were not deceived by the giants neither did the impregnable walls of Jericho cause them a shift of focus.

Numbers 14: 7-8, *"The land, which we passed through to search it, is an exceeding good land. If the Lord delights in us,* *then he will bring us into this land, and give it us, a land which floweth with milk and honey."*

They were not moved by the size of the people they saw in that land. They were sure of their position in God Almighty, no wonder both of them were the only two amongst the multitudes who left Egypt that stepped into the Promised Land.

Joshua having realised the secret of proper positioning in God and its benefits initiated his whole family into it. Joshua actually succeeded Moses and presided over the allotment of inheritance to the Israelites.

Joshua 24: 15, *"...Choose you this day whom ye will serve...BUT as for me and my house, we will serve the Lord."*

Little wonder the Lord stood by him as he fought and conquered the Israelites' enemies in battles. The sun and the moon actually stood still for a whole day on account of him...a Prince commanded it to be so.

Ecclesiastes 8:4-5, *"Where the word of a king is, there is power and who may say unto him, what doest thou? Whoso keepeth the commandment shall feel no evil thing: and a wise man's heart discerneth both time and judgment."*

The King begat the Prince, if the word of the king has

power and authority then the words of a Prince carries same.

Caleb on his path did not weaver in his stand with God even in his old age his gaze remained fixed on God.

Once you are rightly positioned, every other thing falls into place. Your strength is renewed and your cup of blessings always filled to overflowing. You will not lack because the Lord is your Shepherd.

The pauper doesn't know his make up because he is imbalanced. He attempts a thousand and one thing at a time yet fails in all of them. The pauper's condition is pitiable; he lacks divine direction and backup.

God guides and directs those who walk in obedience to His instructions. God does not pay for the labour he didn't assign. He will only equip you for the battle in which He is the Commander.

Paupers usually stand-alone, nobody wants to be identified with a failure, a square peg in a round hole. Failure truly is an orphan.

The pauper lacks boldness, speed, stability and success. He has no right standing with God. He is incompetent, his level of education and information notwithstanding.

The paupers are around us; in our churches, work places, homes etc. They live with us, we see them daily. They tell you in flawless and impeccable English accent *"Cool it, I know what I want."*

But knowing what you want isn't all there is, the ultimate is knowing and walking in God`s perfect will for you.

You can walk in God`s perfect will when you have had an encounter with Him. This happens when you humble yourself before the Lord and open your heart to Him sincerely. Acknowledge you are tired of being away from Him and have returned home to Him.

He will give you a new name, a new status and a treasured position. Your life will become meaningful, you will move from grass to grace, from zero to hero. He will change your story from that of a failure to a genius; take you from obscurity to limelight. God can do it.

He created you for the good life and has good thoughts for you. Do not limit Him with your unbelief and self- consciousness. He is waiting for you to respond to His invitation, you won't keep Him waiting forever, will you? There is really nothing you gain from being a pauper rather you loose everything. Accept His invitation and learn to speak the *Princely language!*

"Your action is the product of your thought and your thought is influenced by the source of your inspiration, information and ideas."
- Agu Jaachynma N.E.

Chapter Two

Coping With Life`s Issues

In Chapter one of this book, we saw the plight of a pauper; he lacks several things including direction, proper placement and divine provision. He struggles for everything inspite of God's plans and provisions for him to be abundantly supplied daily. He is like a baby who cries for everything he needs when he could simply call on someone to give him attention, water, food and care.

The pauper struggles for everything, he worries for the now, he panics for tomorrow and he is afraid of the future.

Mathew 6:25-34, *"…Take no thought for your life, what ye shall eat or what ye shall drink, nor yet for your body, what ye shall put on… Take therefore no thought for the morrow, for the morrow shall take thought for the things of itself. Sufficient unto the day is the evil thereof."*

God is committed to meeting the needs of all princes as stated in **Philippians 4:19** *"And my God shall supply all your need according to his riches in glory by Christ Jesus."*

But, this is not true for the pauper; he toils so much and brings in so little, he wakes up early, goes to bed late without achieving much. His pathetic success is never lasting; the Scripture describes his success thus: *"I have seen the wicked in great power and spreading himself like a green bay tree. Yet he passed away, and lo, he was not: yea, I sought him, but he could not be found."* (**Psalm 37:35-36)**

The Pauper thinks no good thoughts, he is self-seeking and has no time to seek the face of the Lord. He doesn't bother about prayers; he does his things as he likes. All he thinks of is *"how do I get the latest Car, House, Clothes, etc".* He is always in competition with people around him even when there is no need for such.

His uses the wrong diction because that's all he has in his collection. He patterns his life after mere mortals. His purpose for making money is to earn a living rather than make a giving.

He manoeuvres his ways and gets his things done by hook or by crook and not by book.

Even in Bible days, they existed. They prefer cutting corners to get what they want.

In the Book of Joshua, we read about Achan - a

pauper, a greedy man who wanted every good thing for selfish consumption at all cost. He was self-centred and cared less for the consequences of his actions to his family members, neighbours and the whole community of Israel.

Joshua 7:20-22, *"And Achan answered Joshua and said, indeed, I have sinned against the Lord God of Israel, and thus have I done: when I saw among the spoils a goody Babylonish garment and two hundred shekels of silver, and a wedge of gold of fifty shekel weight, then I coveted them, and took them and behold, they are hid in the earth in the midst of my tent; and the silver under it."*

Achan, of course, was destroyed together with his family, he perished with the items he coveted, stole but never enjoyed.

Another pauper in the Bible was King Ahab, though king of Isreal yet was not content with all he had; he desired the plot of land belonging to Naboth, a poor citizen in his kingdom. He murdered the poor man and collected his inheritance by force.

1ˢᵗ Kings 21: 2-20 *"...And Ahab spake unto Naboth, saying, Give me thy vineyard, that I may have it for a garden of herbs, because it is near unto my house... And Jezebel his wife* *said unto him, I will give thee the vineyard of Naboth the Jezreelite...Then they sent to Jezebel, saying, Naboth is stoned, and is dead...And Ahab said to Elijah, hast thou found me, O mine enemy? And he answered, I have found thee; because thou hast sold thyself to work evil in the sight of the LORD."*

The common things with these are desperation and selfishness. They do not have the fruits of the Holy Spirit rather they manifest the works of the flesh. They have no genuine love for anyone around them; they are only concerned about themselves.

A pauper can go to any length to get what he wants not minding its destructive consequences and not bothering about what the next person feels about his actions.

Another common attribute with the paupers is shortsightedness or immediate gratification. They do not see ahead, they do not think ahead, all that matter to them is now! They want what gives them satisfaction now albeit temporarily.

They kill or maim innocent people in the process of their wanton pursuits and aren't bothered about the long-term rewards of their actions.

Every of their action stems from impatience, intolerance and falsehood. Although things may look fine and good for them outwardly, but in the long run they are losers.

Years ago, I knew of a young woman who was involved in an illicit affair with a married man. The man's family did all they could to stop the lady from disrupting the peace in the young man's home to no avail. When I learnt of it and confronted her, she told me she was upset because the young man was already giving their relationship a cold shoulder. *"That is good, let him go so you can have a better life,"* I said to her. The response I got from her went thus: *"My dear, please keep your advice to yourself, as for that man, he is my toy and I must keep him by hook or by crook. Even if he leaves me now, he must come back to me; he must come crawling on his knees to beg me."*

I was shocked as I heard the voice of wickedness and desperation speaking through her. Majority of the paupers are frantic in their bids, they always act in frustration. They pursue ambition instead of vision, they want to be *"christians"* instead of children of God. They choose to answer *"Prophets"* instead of God's messengers; they will do everything to bear the tag millionaires instead of tapping from the abundance of God's wealth and riches.

They lack purpose and divine direction either because they did not ask for it or because they asked for the wrong reasons.

They do not seek godly counsel but venture into projects because someone else did it and made a huge success out of it. They are always panicky, confused and in a haste . They don't realise that desperation leads to temptation and temptation when not properly handled leads to destruction.

James 1:13-15, *"Let no man say when he is tempted, I am tempted of God for God cannot be tempted with evil, neither tempteth he any man. But every man is tempted when he is drawn away of his own lust, and enticed. Then when lust hath conceived, it bright forth sin, and sin when justified, bringeth forth death."*

The pauper is vulnerable to pride and pride destroys man's glory. Pride sets man against God for God resists the proud but gives grace to the humble.

The *"humble"* are the Princes of God, they do not walk in darkness but seek and discover God's purpose for their lives. The princes equally walk with God every step of the way in accomplishing their purpose. They seek God`s wisdom and with this wisdom, they do exploits.

James 3:17-18, *"But the wisdom that is from above is first pure, then peaceable, gentle and easy to be entreated, full of mercy and good fruits without partiality and without hypocrisy. And the fruit of righteousness is sown in peace of them that make peace."*

A relationship with this Wisdom from above will make life easier and thrilling for anyone that partakes of it. God desires everyone to receive this Wisdom hence this invitation: *"Come unto me, all ye that labour and are heavy laden and I will give you rest. Take my yoke upon you and learn of me, for I am meek and lowly in heart and ye shall find rest unto your souls. For my yoke is easy and my burden is light."* (**Matthew 11: 28-30**)

Anyone who accepts this invitation and endorses it is made for life, it does not matter where such a person has been, what counts is what he is doing with the truth of God's word.

The pauper, the wicked, the downtrodden, anybody can come in response to this invitation and their lives will be given a lift and a new meaning. Something interesting about God is He never meets you and leaves you at the spot where He met you rather He takes you higher.

Jesus told His disciples when He chose them, *"Follow me and I will make you fishers of men." (**Mathew 4:18-19**)*

From the above verse, the word – *make* means to transform somebody or something into something else. God **makes** those who follow Him and do His word. He changes peoples' statuses and delivers them to their estates. His love is unconditional but His blessings are for those who do His Word. To experience the fullness of His blessings, you must align yourself to the dictates of His Kingdom.

There are systematic principles of growing in grace and in the wisdom of God. You do not try to *"help"* God in any way. Yours is to yield to His words by faith for He has perfected all that concerns you. The first step in yielding to Him and walking in His wisdom is by accepting Jesus Christ into your life.

Life without Christ is catastrophic. The pauper remains stagnated because he has rejected the gift of God to man in the Person of Christ. Christ makes the difference. The pauper cannot experience real pleasure and good life because these things are only found at the right hand of God.

God is the Source, Jesus Christ is the Socket and the Holy Spirit is the Current. Anyone who is not connected to the Source through Jesus Christ will not have the required Current needed for energy output. Furthermore, one who is not consistent with the principles of the Gospel will definitely have partial contact. He will truly not enjoy life.

Life for the pauper, the unbeliever, the wicked is not fun, he toils for everything. The Grace of our Lord Jesus Christ is far from him, the favour of God is lacking and he has no fellowship with the Holy Spirit. He tries to patch up with his human strength but it fails too for *"By strength shall no man prevail."*

Zechariah 4:6, *"Not by might, nor by power but by my Spirit saith the Lord of Hosts."*

Human strength is nothing to lean on; any success procured via this means is temporary and frustrating. The pauper most of the time achieves success through human or satanic influence. This kind of success is short-lived; no wonder we have many *"former this and former that in our societies."*

The pauper does not bother himself about divine success because he is not qualified for it. He centres his mind on the human success which is selfish, ungodly and short-lived.

The satanic success is acquired through killings, maiming and cheating. It doesn't last. Nothing good originates from the devil. Everything he does is a counterfeit of God's blessings.

God's blessings are original; they are not photocopies and that is why for every genuine child of God has a specific instruction, purpose, plan and objective for his life.

The children of God cannot afford to live like the paupers, the impoverished, the sinners and the beggarly elements.

God is explicit and plain about His plans for His children. There is an assignment and a detailed programme for every of His child - those whom He foreknew, predestined, called, justified, glorified and changed their stories.

God is a God of purpose. He doesn't dabble into

things; He doesn't use trial and error method. His ways are sure, they may be slow but they are always sure. Anyone that follows Him never gets stranded on the way.

John 14:6, *"Jesus saith unto him, I am the way, the truth and the life, no man cometh unto the father but by me."*

He is not one of the ways, He is not a way. He is THE WAY, THE TRUTH AND THE LIFE. Anyone going to the Father must pass through Him.

Why do we go to the Father? Must everyone go to the Father? Yes, going to the Father is not optional if you must make an impact (*positively*) in your generation, if you must live and not just exist, then you must go to the Father.

He is the Source; if you must be resourceful you must get connected to Him.

He is the Teacher; if you must learn to live and overcome, you must go to Him. You must go to God if you really want to experience the state of being comfortable and comforted.

2nd Corinthians 1:3-4, " *Blessed be God, even the Father of our Lord Jesus Christ, the Father of mercies, and the God of* *all comfort; Who comforteth us in all our tribulation, that we may be able to comfort them which are in any trouble, by the comfort wherewith we ourselves are comforted of God."*

He is the God of all comfort, if you must be comfortable in life, if you must be comforted in distressing situations you must go to Him.

He is the Solution to every ugly situation, if you must come out of that pit of despair you must come to Him.

Does He discriminate? No, He is the Father of mercy as well. Those that come unto Him, He will in no wise cast out, He is a Rewarder of them that diligently seek Him and those that seek Him early find Him. Is He strong enough to deliver the oppressed? Yes, for He sent His healing word and and delivered them from their destructions.

No man can achieve success without God. Any life without God is doomed and any life without Christ ends in crisis. God is not an option and He doesn't have alternatives. God is in His own class; He is the Author of all good things.

It takes Him nothing to change the status of a man,

the question is *"are you willing and obedient?"*

Isaiah 1:19, *"If ye be willing and obedient, ye shall eat the good of the land."*

Victory on every side is part of the good of the land promised the *"willing and the obedient."*

Remember, victory does not come to cowards; it comes to the brave. Stories abound of those who almost made it to the top but crumbled because of unbelief, fear and doubt.

Lot's wife in the Bible is an example of one who destroyed a great destiny her because of fear, doubt and unbelief. She did not believe that God who rescued them from that land of filthiness and immorality is strong enough to meet their needs and provide all they require. **Genesis 19:26**, *"But his wife looked back from behind him, and she became a pillar of salt."*

Some people are discouraged because of their past lifestyle, a lot others think they have dwelled in a particular pit of undesirable lifestyle for too long and so will not be able to come out to shine forth their light. They have several obstacles distracting them from being mentally or spiritually resourceful.

To such people, I say, if you don't allow your past to pass away, you will pass away with your past. A knockdown will never be a knockout unless you allow it. The reason you are still on and moving is because God is not through with you yet.

What lies ahead of you is better than what you have already experienced. Don't create regrets out of your trials in the past; make real testimonies out of them. The past is indeed irreparable therefore allow it to go, focus on the future for it has lots of good things in stock for you. Forget the past, think of the future, remember God's goodness and His ability to take you over in life, He will establish you if you allow Him.

There are those who live in their past glory and relish their achievements; they lack the persuasion to go for more. They prefer basking in the euphoria of their past glory forgetting that *"the largest room in this life is the room for improvement; if you did it well yesterday nothing stops you from doing it better today and perfecting it tomorrow. If you did it yesterday, that's a clear indication that you can still do more today."* There many people in this class, the class of limitation, the class of the mediocrity.

They get contented with what they managed to

achieve years back, they sit back pulling their beards and rubbing their stomachs saying *"Ten years ago I did this and that."* My question to such folks is *"now, what are you doing to update your success and achievements?"* Remember achievement is like a well-prepared pot of soup, if you do not preserve it well, it will get sour. Achievements can become obsolete and stink if you don't improve on them.

The life of Caleb in the Bible should motivate such people; he never rested on his achievements but kept on until he got all allotments for him and his descendants.

Joshua 14:10-11, *"And now, behold the Lord hath kept me alive, as he said, these forty and five years, even since the Lord spoke this word to Moses... as yet I am as strong this day as I was in the day that Moses sent me: as my strength was then even so is my strength now, for war, both to go out and come."*

His story shows he knew what he wanted to make out of life and not one who didn't know what life will make out of him.

Do not be among those who just pass through life without life passing through them. Don't yield and succumb yourself to life's pressures; don't leave your life to chance. When you do, it indicates you are visionless and a pauper!

A strong man does not succumb to pressures, he overcomes them for he knows that within every pressure is an outflow of pleasure. I advise you to welcome pressure and challenges for they awaken the sleeping giants in you! A strong man takes a firm hold on life and determines to live it out, live it through and overcome it. Don't remain stagnant in any good or bad position.

Christ died for you at Calvary; He paid the price needed for your freedom. He is your Saviour and if you can believe and confess His Lordship over your life, He will change your story and re-write your destiny. Believing and confessing His Lordship over your life are the keys you need to set you on upward motion always!

Your story as a pauper can change today if you yield yourself to God and accept the change He has made available for you in Christ Jesus. People succeed not only because they are destined to, but also because they are determined to. Everyone is destined to succeed but only few are determined. Those who received their dreams, desired, deserved and worked for them!

You cannot do it all alone; there is no magic on how a pauper as impoverished as he finds himself can cope with life's issues all alone. He needs the Saviour to save him, he needs the Guardian to guide and guard him, he needs the Comforter to comfort him and the Teacher to teach him.

God leads those who are yielded to His instructions; He can only send you when He has trained you. Make yourself available for Him today. God can handle your shattered, scattered and battered destiny with His power and ability. He can suture any future no matter how ruptured or punctured it might be.

There is no life so corrupted and disrupted that the Master Planner, the Creator cannot correct, reconstruct and connect rightly. All you need do is answer the call to cease from your own activities. Jesus said, *"Come unto Me all ye that labour and are heavy laden and I will give you rest."* **(Mathew 11:28)**.

Don't die a pauper, don't die a commoner and a weakling. Be encouraged, make the desired move today, and change your status!

"When you go after your vision with Divine instinct, success becomes inevitable."
                    - Agu Jaachynma N.E.

Chapter Three

The Emergence of the Prince

God the Father desired to have the world reconciled to Him as it was in the beginning before the serpent deceived the first Adam. God covenanted with Abraham but Abraham did not measure up to the standard, He tried Noah and it did not work out perfectly, He motioned to Moses and it ended in disaster.

He wanted fellowship and sweet communion with man, He longed for His Spirit to still dwell amongst men. He spoke forth His Word to a virgin called Mary through Angel Gabriel and she conceived and delivered God`s Word to save man.

The birth of God`s Word was prophesied about by Isaiah in the Old Testament, the prophecy came to fulfilment in the New Testament. Here is Isaiah`s prophecy concerning the Word of God made flesh: *Isaiah 9:6*, *"For unto us a child is born, unto us a Son is given... and his Name shall be called Wonderful Counsellor, the Mighty God, the Everlasting Father, the Prince of Peace..."*

God`s Word is His Spirit and His answer to man`s

challenges.

The Word of the Lord, the Spirit of the Most High was birthed physically as the Prince of Peace. He came to reconcile man to God. He came to change the stories and destinies of men; He came to give man life in abundance, yes, He came to set the captives free!

He came to restore the sweet communion between God and mankind. He has been in existence from the beginning, from creation; He existed as the Word in God's System. He did not come forth until the appointed time - the time that God spoke Him forth through the Virgin Mary.

John 1:1- 2 says: *"In the beginning was the WORD and the WORD was with God and the WORD was God. The same was in the beginning with God."*

Because it wasn't yet the appointed time, we saw Him before His birth but did not recognize Him. We did not give Him attention for we didn't know who He was. **John 1: 10-11** says, *"He was in the world, and the world was made by him, and the world knew him not. He came unto his own, and his own received him not."*

Yet He is the Word of God. Here is His curriculum vitae all through the Scriptures:

In *Genesis,* we saw Him as the **Seed of the Woman** that will bruise the serpent's head, *"And I will put enmity between thee and the woman, and between thy seed and her seed; it shall bruise thy head, and thou shalt bruise his heel."* (**Genesis 3:15**)

In *Exodus,* we saw Him as the **Passover Lamb** without blemish, *"Your lamb shall be without blemish, a male of the first year:..."* (**Exodus 12:5**)

In *Leviticus,* He was the **Fire of the Lord** that consumed the burnt offerings of the people to the Lord, *"And there came a fire out from before the* LORD, *and consumed upon the altar the burnt offering and the fat: which when all the people saw, they shouted, and fell on their faces."* (**Leviticus 9: 24**)

In *Numbers,* He appeared as the **Countenance of God** that gave the Israelites peace, *"The* LORD *lift up his countenance upon thee, and give thee peace"* (**Numbers 6: 26**). He was also the **Cloud of the Lord** upon them by day, *"And the cloud of the* LORD *was upon them by day,* *when they went out of the camp." (**Numbers 10:34**)*

In *Deuteronomy*, we saw Him as the **Commandment and the Name of the Lord** *which* the people of the Earth shall see and fear, *"And all people of the earth shall see that thou art called by the name of the LORD; and they shall be afraid of thee." (**Deuteronomy 28:10**)*

In *Joshua*, He was **The Book of the Law** *Spoken and written by God* that should not depart out of our mouth but shall give us good success, *"This book of the law shall not depart out of thy mouth; but thou shalt meditate therein day and night, that thou mayest observe to do according to all that is written therein: for then thou shalt make thy way prosperous, and then thou shalt have good success." (**Joshua 1:8**)*

In *Judges*, we saw Him as the **Palm tree of Deborah** between Ramah and Bethel where the judge sits and obtains wisdom to judge cases, *"And she dwelt under the palm tree of Deborah between Ramah and Bethel in mount Ephraim: and the children of Israel came up to her for judgment." (**Judges 4:5**)*

In *Ruth*, we saw Him as **Boaz** *who came from Bethlehem* to give hope unto the hopeless and gave help to the

55

needy, our Kinsman indeed, *"And, behold, Boaz came from Bethlehem, and said unto the reapers, The LORD be with you. And they answered him, The LORD bless thee." (**Ruth 2:4**)*

In *1ˢᵗ Samuel*, He was the **Voice of God** that called Samuel and declare the mind of God to the little boy, *"That the LORD called Samuel: and he answered, Here am I."* (**1ˢᵗ Samuel 3:4-14**)

In *2ⁿᵈ Samuel*, we saw Him as the **Power of God** that turned Ahithophel's Counsel to foolishness, to allow God's people dominion over the enemy, *"And one told David, saying, Ahithophel is among the conspirators with Absalom. And David said, O LORD, I pray thee, turn the counsel of Ahithophel into foolishness."* (**2 Samuel 15:31**)

In *1ˢᵗ Kings*, He came as the **Wisdom of God** upon King Solomon that distinguished him from all other rulers, *"Give therefore thy servant an understanding heart to judge thy people, that I may discern between good and bad: for who is able to judge this thy so great a people? And the speech pleased the LORD, that Solomon had asked this thing."* (**1ˢᵗ Kings 3:9-10**)

In *2ⁿᵈ Kings*, He was the **Hand of God** that came

upon Prophet Elisha and caused him to do greater works than Elijah his predecessor, "...*that the hand of the* LORD *came upon him.*" (**2 Kings 3:15**)

In *1ˢᵗ Chronicles*, He appeared as the **Favour of God** upon Jabez that changed Jabez story and destiny completely, "*And Jabez called on the God of Israel, saying, Oh that thou wouldest bless me indeed, and enlarge my coast, and that thine hand might be with me, and that thou wouldest keep me from evil, that it may not grieve me! And God granted him that which he requested.*" (**1ˢᵗ Chronicles 4:10**)

In *2ⁿᵈ Chronicles*, we saw Him as the **Glory of the Lord** that filled the temple, which Solomon built and dedicated unto God, "*...and the glory of the* LORD *filled the house.*" (**2ⁿᵈ Chronicles 7:1**)

In *Ezra*, He was the **Strength of God** upon Zerubbabel and Joshua that caused them to rebuild the temple of God without assistance from the infidel, "*But Zerubbabel, and Jeshua, and the rest of the chief of the fathers of Israel, said unto them, Ye have nothing to do with us to build an house unto our God; but we ourselves together will build unto the* LORD *God of Israel, as king Cyrus the king of Persia hath commanded us.*" (**Ezra 4:3**)

In *Nehemiah*, He came as the **Book of the Law** that Ezra and Nehemiah read to the people of Israel, *"So they read in the book in the law of God distinctly, and gave the sense, and caused them to understand the reading."* **(Nehemiah 8:8)**

In *Esther*, He is the **Mordecai of the seed of the Jew** whom Haman could not prevail against, *"... If Mordecai be of the seed of the Jews, before whom thou hast begun to fall, thou shalt not prevail against him, but shalt surely fall before him."* **(Esther 6:13)**

In *Job*, He is **our Redeemer that liveth** and who shall stand at the later day upon the earth, *"For I know that my redeemer liveth,..."* **(Job 19: 25)**

In *Psalms*, He is **our Shepherd** and for His Name's sake we shall not want, *"The LORD is my shepherd; I shall not want."* **(Psalm 23:1)**

In *Proverbs*, He appeared as the **Wisdom of God** *that was set up from everlasting,* from the beginning, or ever the earth was, *"I wisdom dwell with prudence,... I was set up from everlasting, from the beginning, or ever the earth was."* **(Proverbs 8:12, 23)**

In *Ecclesiastes*, He came as the **Word of the king** *that comes with power* in it. None can ask him what he does!, *"Where the word of a king is, there is power: and who may say unto him, What doest thou?"* (**Ecclesiastes 8: 4**)

In *Songs of Solomon*, He is the **Rose of Sharon, the Lily of the valleys,** *"I am the rose of Sharon, and the lily of the valleys."* (**Song of Solomon 2:1**)

In *Isaiah*, He is the Sign called **Immanuel,** *"Therefore the Lord himself shall give you a sign; Behold, a virgin shall conceive, and bear a son, and shall call his name Immanuel."* (**Isaiah 7:14**)

In *Jeremiah*, we saw Him as **our Potter, the Righteous branch** whose name is the Lord our Righteousness, *"Behold, the days come, saith the LORD, that I will raise unto David a righteous Branch, and a King shall reign and prosper, and shall execute judgment and justice in the earth. In his days Judah shall be saved, and Israel shall dwell safely: and this is his name whereby he shall be called, THE LORD OUR RIGHTEOUSNESS."* (**Jeremiah 23:5-6**)

In the *Book of Lamentations*, He is the **Lord's mercies** that stops us from being consumed, *the Lord's compassion* that fail not *"It is of the LORD's mercies that we* *are not consumed, because his compassions fail not."* (**Lamentations 3:22**)

In the *Book of Ezekiel*, He came to us as the **Word of God** *spoken by Prophet Ezekiel* that caused the dry bones to live! "*… Prophesy upon these bones, and say unto them, O ye dry bones, hear the word of the* LORD." (**Ezekiel 37:4**)

In the *Book of Daniel*, He was the **Fourth Man** *in Nebuchadnezzar's furnace* who came to comfort and rescue God's children, "*… and the form of the fourth is like the Son of God."* (**Daniel 3: 25**)

In the *Book of Hosea*, He came as our **Faithful and Loving Husband** who allures and brings us into the wilderness to speak comfortably unto us *"Therefore, behold, I will allure her, and bring her into the wilderness, and speak comfortably unto her."* (**Hosea 2:14**)

In the *Book of Joel*, He is our **Restorer** that will restore to us the lost and wasted years, *"And I will restore to you the years that the locust hath eaten, the cankerworm, and the caterpiller, and the palmerworm, my great army which I sent among you."* (**Joel 2:25**)

In the *Book of Amos*, He is **the One that maketh the seven stars and Orion** and turneth shadow of death into the morning that we are advised to seek, "*Seek him that maketh the seven stars and Orion, and turneth the shadow of death into the morning, and maketh the day dark with night: that calleth for the waters of the sea, and poureth them out upon the face of the earth: The* LORD *is his name.*" (***Amos 5:8***)

In *Obadiah*, we saw Him as **our *Deliverer*** that dwells upon Mount Zion, "*But upon mount Zion shall be deliverance, and there shall be holiness; and the house of Jacob shall possess their possessions.*" (***Obadiah 1:17***)

In the *Book of Jonah*, He was **the *Word*** *that came unto the King of Nineveh* and caused him to rise from his throne, "*For word came unto the king of Nineveh, and he arose from his throne, and he laid his robe from him, and covered him with sackcloth, and sat in ashes.*" (***Jonah 3:6***)

In the *Book of Micah*, He was **the *Ruler from Bethlehem*** whose going forth have been from of old, from everlasting, "*But thou, Bethlehem Ephratah, though thou be little among the thousands of Judah, yet out of thee shall he come forth unto me that is to be ruler in Israel; whose goings forth have been from of old, from everlasting.*" (***Micah 5:2***)

In the *Book of Nahum*, He is **the *Feet of him that bringeth good tidings and publisheth peace***, *"Behold upon the mountains the feet of him that bringeth good tidings, that publisheth peace! O Judah, keep thy solemn feasts, perform thy vows: for the wicked shall no more pass through thee; he is utterly cut off."* (**Nahum 1:15**)

In *Habakkuk*, He is **the *Vision*** *that* God gave to Habakkuk, which is for an appointed time, *"And the* LORD *answered me…Write the vision, and make it plain upon tables, that he may run that readeth it. For the vision is yet for an appointed time…though it tarry, wait for it; because it will surely come, it will not tarry."* (**Habakkuk 2:2-3**)

In *Zephaniah*, He is **the *Name and the Praise*** that God promise to make us among the people of the earth, *"At that time will I bring you again, even in the time that I gather you: for I will make you a name and a praise among all people of the earth, when I turn back your captivity before your eyes, saith the* LORD." (**Zephaniah 3: 20**)

In *Haggai*, He is **the *Glory of the latter house*** that will surpass the former, *"The glory of this latter house shall be greater than of the former, saith the* LORD *of hosts: and in this place will I give peace, saith the* LORD *of hosts."*

(Haggai 2:9)

In *Zechariah*, He is **the *Wall of fire*** round about us and the Glory of God in our midst, *"For I, saith the LORD, will be unto her a wall of fire round about, and will be the glory in the midst of her."* **(Zechariah 2:5)**

In the *Book of Malachi* He is **the *Godly seed*** that couples are advised to seek, *"And did not he make one? Yet had he the residue of the spirit. And wherefore one? That he might seek a godly seed. Therefore take heed to your spirit, and let none deal treacherously against the wife of his youth."* **(Malachi 2:15)**

In *Matthew*, **He is *Christ, the Son of the living God,*** *"...Thou art the Christ, the Son of the living God."* **(Matthew 16:16)**

In *Mark*, He is **the *Good Master*** that makes His followers, *"And Jesus said unto them, Come ye after me, and I will make you to become fishers of men."* **(Mark 1:17)**

In *Luke*, **He is *Jesus, the Son of the Highest*,** *"...shalt call his name JESUS. He shall be great, and shall be called the Son of the Highest: ..."* **(Luke 1:31,32)**

In *John*, He is **the *True Vine*,** *"I am the true vine, and my Father is the husbandman."* (***John 15:1***)

In *Acts of the Apostles*, He is **the *Just One*,** *"Which of the prophets have not your fathers persecuted? and they have slain them which shewed before of the coming of the Just One; of whom ye have been now the betrayers and murderers:"* (**Acts of Apostles 7: 52**)

In *Romans*, He is **the *Resurrected Christ*,** *"Therefore we are buried with him by baptism into death: that like as Christ was raised up from the dead by the glory of the Father, even so we also should walk in newness of life."* (***Romans 6:4***)

In *1ˢᵗ Corinthians*, **He is *Christ the Power and the Wisdom of God*,** *"...Christ the power of God, and the wisdom of God."* (***1ˢᵗ Corinthians 1:24***)

In *2ⁿᵈ Corinthians*, He is **the *Image of God*** that shines unto us, *"In whom the god of this world hath blinded the minds of them which believe not, lest the light of the glorious gospel of Christ, who is the image of God, should shine unto them."* (***2ⁿᵈ Corinthians 4: 4***)

In *Galatians*, He is **the *Son of God*** who loved us and

gave Himself for us. *"…but Christ liveth in me: and the life which I now live in the flesh I live by the faith of the Son of God, who loved me, and gave himself for me."* (**Galatians 2:20**)

In *Ephesians*, **He is Christ the head of the Church,** *"…even as Christ is the head of the church: and he is the saviour of the body."* (**Ephesians 5: 23**)

In *Philippians*, He is **the One that has the Name above every other name,** whose Name commands worship, reverence, etc., *"Wherefore God also hath highly exalted him, and given him a name which is above every name: That at the name of Jesus every knee should bow, of things in heaven, and things in earth, and things under the earth;"* (**Philippians 2:9-10**)

In *Colossians*, He is **Christ in us the hope of glory,** *"…which is Christ in you, the hope of glory."* (**Colossians 1:27**)

In *1st Thessalonians*, He is **the Faithful one** that has called us and who will also fulfil His promises to us, *"Faithful is he that calleth you,…"* (**1st Thessalonians 5:24**)

In *2nd Thessalonians*, He is **the *Lord of Peace*** who will give us peace by all means, "*Now the Lord of peace himself give you peace always by all means...*" (***2nd Thessalonians 3:16***)

In *1st Timothy*, He **is the only *Mediator*** between God and us, "*For there is one God, and one mediator between God and men, the man Christ Jesus.*" (***1st Timothy 2:5***)

In *2nd Timothy*, He is of ***the Seed of David*** that was raised from dead, "*Remember that Jesus Christ of the seed of David was raised from the dead according to my gospel.*" (***2nd Timothy 2:8***)

In the *Book of Titus*, He is ***Jesus Christ our Saviour,*** "*...Jesus Christ our Saviour.*" (***Titus 3:6***)

In *Philemon*, He is **the *Christ Jesus*** *through whom we have every good thing*, "*That the communication of thy faith may become effectual by the acknowledging of every good thing which is in you in Christ Jesus.*" (***Philemon 1:6***)

In the *Book of Hebrews*, He is **the *Heir of all things*,** *the Brightness of His Glory, the Express Image of God's person*, "*...whom he hath appointed heir of all things, ...Who being the brightness of his glory, and the express image of his* person, and upholding all things by the word of his power, when he had by himself purged our sins, sat down on the right hand of the Majesty on high." (**Hebrews 1:2-3**)

In the *Book of James*, He is **our Lord** that has promised us the crown of life, "*Blessed is the man that endureth temptation: for when he is tried, he shall receive the crown of life, which the Lord hath promised to them that love him.*" (***James 1:12***)

In *1ˢᵗ Peter*, He is **the Shepherd and Bishop** of our souls, "*For ye were as sheep going astray; but are now returned unto the Shepherd and Bishop of your souls.*" (**1ˢᵗ Peter 2:25**)

In *2ⁿᵈ Peter*, He is ***the Lord** who is not slack concerning His promises to us,* who lives in a frame of timelessness, "*The Lord is not slack concerning his promise, as some men count slackness; but is longsuffering to us-ward, not willing that any should perish, but that all should come to repentance.*" (***2ⁿᵈ Peter 3:9***)

In *1ˢᵗ John*, He is **the Eternal life** that God has given us, he that has Him has life and he that has Him not has no eternal life, "*And this is the record, that God hath given to us eternal life, and this life is in his Son.*" (***1ˢᵗ John 5:11,12***)

In *2nd John*, He is **the Son of the Father** *in Truth and love*, "*Grace be with you, mercy, and peace, from God the Father, and from the Lord Jesus Christ, the Son of the Father, in truth and love.*" (**2nd John 3**)

In *3rd John*, He is **the Friend** *who delights so much in our divine health and prosperity*, "*Beloved, I wish above all things that thou mayest prosper and be in health, even as thy soul prospereth.*" (**3rd John 2**)

In the *General Epistle of Jude*, He is **the One that is able to keep us from falling** and present us faultless before the presence of God's glory, "*Now unto him that is able to keep you from falling, and to present you faultless before the presence of his glory with exceeding joy,*" (**Jude 1:24**)

In the *Revelation of Saint John the Divine*, He is **the Alpha and the Omega,** the *Beginning and the Ending* which was, is and is to come, "*I am Alpha and Omega, the beginning and the ending, saith the Lord, which is, and which was, and which is to come, the Almighty*" (**Revelation 1:8**)

He came for a purpose, at the fullness of God's time, He emerged and when His assignment was duly completed. He left and right now sits at the right hand of God the Father, mediating for other numerous princes who have remained paupers as a result of ignorance.

When He came, He did not go bragging about Himself or flaunting His identity, no, He made Himself of low reputation and took the position of a servant. He knew there was a price tag to His purpose and He willingly paid all.

It was not all milk and honey; sometimes He had to go alone into the mountains to pray, commune with God and receive strength, instructions and directions to move on successfully.

At other times He went to the temple to teach the people the way of the Lord and equally led them by example. He bare the peoples' burdens; when they were hungry He fed them, when they were ill He healed them. He turned their sorrows and mourning into dancing. When confused and lost direction, He instilled in them teachings of hope and gave them a sense of direction.

He accomplished His mission; His emergence was planned and timely for God is a God of purpose.

Jesus while on earth met man's needs and showed them the Way to the Father.

He was not like any of the prophets. His mission was not to live out an ambition, no, He was destined for a vision and that vision perfected His mission on earth. He was always found at the right place at the right time.

When an adulterous Samaritan woman needed to be saved, Jesus went to the well to meet with her. When a couple was nearly embarrassed on their wedding day for lack of wine, He saved them from the humiliation.

He supplied the needs of all who came to Him. Once the Pharisees were about stoning an adulterous woman, Jesus appeared on the scene and rescued her from perishing.

The story of this woman never ceases to amaze me, she was caught in adultery they said; where was her partner? Does one commit adultery alone? They dragged this helpless woman round the city because she had none to speak up for her.

Probably, her partner in the crime was a prominent person so they didn't want to embarrass him. They refused judging him and preferred dealing with the woman who had none to speak for her . Thank God, Jesus came to her rescue, her sins not counting. She was already condemned and sentenced to death by stoning, those to cast the stones were ready with their stones but the Prince of Life met with her and gave her a brand new song and life.

Jesus is Lord! He came to disarm and *"defeet"* (*defeat*) all your accusers and strip them off all the weapons they have acquired to fight against you and against your destiny. When they are disarmed - left without arms and *"defeeted"* - left without feet, how will they fight you? The Prince of Peace is meeting with you right now at that point where you need peace. The Lord of Hosts is going with you on that journey, so be not afraid!

The Prince came to draw men unto Himself; He came as the **Bread of life** for the hungry, *"I am that bread of life"* (*John 6:48*)

He came as **Living water** for the thirsty, *"Jesus answered and said unto her, If thou knewest the gift of God,* *and who it is that saith to thee, Give me to drink; thou wouldest have asked of him, and he would have given thee living water… Jesus answered and said unto her, Whosoever drinketh of this water shall thirst again: But whosoever drinketh of the water that I shall give him shall never thirst; but the water that I shall give him shall be in him a well of water springing up into everlasting life" (John 4:10 -14).*

"In the last day, that great day of the feast, Jesus stood and cried, saying, If any man thirst, let him come unto me, and drink" (John 7:37)

He came as **Light** unto the people walking in darkness, *"Then spake Jesus again unto them, saying, I am the light of the world: he that followeth me shall not walk in darkness, but shall have the light of life" (John 8: 12)*

The Prince of God is **the Way** – leading and directing God's people to the path of righteousness. *"Jesus saith unto him, I am the way, the truth, and the life: no man cometh unto the Father, but by me" (John 14:6)*

He is **the Truth** of God`s Word. He is the Truth, He does not lie. He came as the Truth to stand against all the lies of the enemy, *"Jesus saith unto him, I am the way, the truth, and the life: no man cometh unto the Father, but by* *me"* (*John 14:6*).

Has He made any promise to you? Hold unto His word, He will fulfil it! Has he spoken anything concerning your situation, He is God and He is truth, He does not lie, He will perfect what He has said concerning you.

The Prince came as **Hope** to the hopeless; He is not only interested in giving your life here on earth a new meaning but also to give you an everlasting life – the life and nature of God.

Jesus came as **the Good Shepherd** to tend you like His lamb, to lead you to quiet and still waters where nothing will disturb your rest and refreshments.

The Prince came as **the only Door** to all the good things of life, no matter what your desires are, He can handle them for you.

3rd John 2 says *"Beloved, I wish above all things that thou mayest prosper and be in health, even as thy soul prospereth."*

Jesus is the Door, through Him, we can obtain

mercy, favour and grace in times of need. Everyone who enters through Him is secured. Jesus really cares!

The Prince came as the only key to answered prayers, for your prayers to produce results; they must be made in His Name.

For your prayer to get result, you have to pray IN THE NAME OF JESUS not THROUGH THE NAME OF JESUS. The reason is because you don't just pass through Him to get to the Father rather you are in Him, standing in His place and having the authority to use His Name.

His Name is the Ultimate. Only prayers made in His Name are effective.

Jesus Christ is the Prince of Peace! He is the Way, the Truth and the Life. His Name is powerful and life giving. His Name brings salvation, answers to prayers and delivers one from shame!

The Prince of Peace does not encourage unrighteous living. Read very carefully the account of the woman with the death penalty hanging on her neck, "*And the scribes and Pharisees brought unto him a woman taken in adultery; and when they had set her in the midst,... So when they continued asking him, he lifted up himself, and said unto them, He that is without sin among you, let him first cast a stone at her…She said, No man, Lord. And Jesus said unto her, Neither do I condemn thee: go, and sin no more"* **(John 8: 3-11)**.

When Christ stooped down to write, I believe He wanted to remind them of this principle *"thou shalt not judge."* He had already told them *"he that is without sin among you, let him first cast a stone at her."* At the word of the Prince, the Holy Spirit swung into action immediately and convicted them of their sins.

I want to believe He was listing the Ten Commandments and the other laws of Moses when He stooped down. The crowd seeing what He was writing realised they were equally guilty of one sin or the other as such weren't worthy to condemn the woman. Ask me how I know: the Bible says, *"They being convicted by their own conscience went out one by one."* What do you think would have sent them away like that?

Jesus wanted them to know that they were not worthy to stone the woman to death as all of them were guilty of the same offence for no sin is greater than the other. The Person who said *"do not steal, equally said do not lie..."*

If Jesus was in support of the woman's offence, He would have asked her to go without any admonition but the Bible said in **John 8: 11**: *"He said, woman, where are thine accusers? Hath no man condemned thee? ... Neither do I condemn thee: go and sin NO MORE."*

Jesus didn't come to condemn us but to call all to repentance for His Father doesn't delight in the death of sinners.

The Prince came to destroy the works of the enemy. He came to draw men unto Himself. He came to teach men how to be successful in life. He came to reconcile man to God. Jesus, the Prince of Peace came to change the battered, tattered, destroyed destiny of man and present man with a new life in Him. He brought the life of focus, the life of vision, the life with a mission, the life that has purpose, goals and objectives. He came to draw man out of darkness and bring him into His marvellous light.

Jesus has not changed. His motives and intent for coming to the world have not been erased. He is still in the business of reconciling man to God, though

THE PRINCE & THE PAUPER

this task is now committed to the hands of the pauper-turned-Princes.

The Prince is still setting captives free; He still heals the sick, saves the lost, repair and restructure destinies.

Will you give Him a chance today? If you don't, it means you want His emergence to be irrelevant in your life. It means you want His sufferings on the Cross of Calvary to be immaterial. It means you are calling bluff the precious blood He poured out on the Cross of Calvary.

Remember the admonition of the prophets of old, *"today, if you hear his voice, harden not your heart"*. Are you inviting Him into your life today? If you are and you sincerely mean it, then say this prayer:

Dear Lord God, I come to you in the Name of Jesus Christ. Your word says, "If I call upon the Name of Jesus I will be saved." I ask Jesus to come into my life and be the Lord of my life. I receive eternal life into my spirit and I declare that I am saved. I am born –again, I am a child of God and Christ now dwells in me. He is reigning now in every facet of my life. Thank you Lord for giving my life a meaning, I now walk in the consciousness of my new life in Christ, Amen.

77

Beloved, congratulations! There is joy in heaven now as a result of what you just did. I tell you, you will never regret it. I took the same decision several years back as a Junior Secondary School student and have never regretted it.

The Spirit of the Lord is resident in you now and henceforth will pilot the affairs of your life, if you let Him.

"God is always on time, He may not arrive when you expect Him to but He never comes late."
-Agu Jaachynma N.E.

Chapter Four

The Prince and the Pauper Meet

The pauper was roaming about aimlessly; he didn't know how to achieve his goals. He walks in confusion, as nothing seemed to be going for him. He was in a dilemma not knowing his left from his right! In the midst of his confusion, he saw Light at the end of the other tunnel, as the Prince emerged and opted to give meaning to the pauper's life.

The pauper deserved to die but the Prince paid the pauper's debts and gave him life. The Prince drank the cup of suffering meant for the pauper and received the lashes that were meant for the pauper's back.

He wore the crown of thorns and carried the cross the pauper should have carried. He set the pauper free. He loosened the bond of wickedness that held the pauper bound. He removed the burden off the pauper's shoulders and the yoke off his neck.

There are different *"pauperic"* levels in life. Jesus identified with them all and paid their penalty. Now, the paupers are free to sing!

*To the **sick and infirmed** paupers, the Prince gave life and made them whole (**1st Peter 2:24**)*

*To the **lost,** He gave words of wisdom, sound teaching and a sense of* *direction (Luke 20).*

To those with **battered and tattered** *self-image, He restructured and sutured their self-esteem (**Luke 13:10-18**).*

The woman talked about in the Scripture above (Luke 13) may have given up the hope of ever standing upright again. She may have believed it was her cross to bear so she accepted it; she may have thought God was responsible for her affliction.

Yet her miracle came when she least expected it, her transformation came at the right time. Her deliverance came her way the moment she met with the Prince. She must have twisted herself sideways and all round to check if it's real or not. She may have smiled, jumped and sang praises to God. Always an encounter with the Prince elicits songs, laughter and dancing from those concerned.

In another instance in the Bible, we read of Lazarus and his sisters, though friends with Jesus yet they experienced challenges. Lazarus got sick, died and they buried him! His sisters were hurt, bitter and pained. They were angry with Jesus for deserting them when they needed Him more. According to man's limited knowledge, Lazarus' case was hopeless for he was not only dead but also buried for four days! His body was already decomposing, there was no iota of hope anywhere but when the Prince emerged, the story changed!

John 11:35 says *"Jesus wept."* Why do you think He wept? Why will the Author of life, the Maker of all things, the Lily of the valley, the Mighty Man in battle, the One who parted the Red Sea weep? Surely, it was not because Lazarus died neither was it because he was long buried and decomposing.

Jesus wept for man's helplessness even with the Helper standing next to him. He wept because He saw the human mind inundated with thoughts of impossibilities; man only saw limitations and hopelessness. Man no longer manifests the glory given to him by God at creation.

Jesus handled the situation, called Lazarus up from the grave, restored man's trust and confidence in God. Jesus turned the sorrows of Lazarus' siblings to joy and laughter.

At another occasion, Jesus met some people going to the cemetery to bury a young man- the only son of a widow. He stopped the pallbearers and restored life to dead young man (**Luke 7:11-18**).

The Prince is always on time, He may not come when you want Him to but He is never late! He may not answer your prayers the way you want Him to but He will always give you the best! Just trust Him! He is the same yesterday, today and forever. He has not changed, He still changes situations and circumstances to the favour of His people.

What the enemy thinks is a breakdown, Jesus changes to a breakthrough. When the enemy presents obstacles to God`s children, Jesus transforms them to stepping-stones. What the enemy positions for our downfall, Jesus turns to be a downpour of blessings. He loves us and always gives us the best!

No situation is too big or too small for Him to handle, no circumstance is too serious for Him to unravel. As we read above, He raised people from dead. He equally fed those whose problems were just hunger. Yea, such trivial things as hunger and thirst also catches His attention.

The point of meeting for the Prince and the pauper was the Cross- where the Prince was made an outcast. He hung naked before the whole world, made a laughing stock and was crucified. He was flogged, rough-handled, humiliated, treated with so much scorn and contempt because of His love for humanity!

The Prince bore punishments for crimes He didn't commit but today the message of His death brings joy, hope and peace to humanity, Halleluiah! The agony He went through now brings upliftment for the lowly, riches and wealth to the pauper and glory to God the Father!

At the cross, there was an exchange of positions...the Prince took the place of the pauper, paid his debt and transformed him. At resurrection, God rewarded and exalted the Prince. God gave Him a Name that is above every other name. Right now, the Prince is in heaven seated at the right hand of God our Father but His exalted Name works for us here on earth.

Whenever His Name is mentioned with revelation and in faith, it brings the fullness of His finished works at Calvary to bear irrespective of the situation and circumstance. The Name of Jesus is not an ordinary Name, Sicknesses tremble at that Name, demons bow to it; the devil takes to his heels at the mention of that Name. Halleluiah! That's the Name we have working for us.

The pauper-turned-prince now uses the name of the Prince to work wonders. The name when called upon in faith heals the sick, raises the dead, sets the captives free, turns situations and circumstances around. His name works wonders.

The pauper's story has changed, his battered image has equally been sutured, his veiled destiny has been unveiled. The pauper's once shattered and scattered future is now glorious through the finished works of the Prince. He nurtured and nourished the bleak, punctured and ruptured future of the pauper. The Pauper's identity has changed, his name is equally changed, God calls him a god and a child of the Most High. Reconciling with God is the most important step in this life of glory; do so today *if you* *haven`t.*

In your walk with God, you do not look back with yearning; your gaze should be on the Author and the Finisher of your faith. *"Remember lot's wife."* (**Luke 17:32**). Jesus counseling his disciples told them: *"No man, having put his hand to the plough, and looking back, is fit for the kingdom of God."* (**Luke 9:62**)

Nobody ever moves faster and steadily looking backwards! The back is past and gone, the past is what Jesus handled at the cross. Now, you should work the Word; change your garment and mindset. Renew your thinking with God`s word. Have nothing to do with life in a dungeon anymore, do not look down on what Christ achieved for you.

Give your self-esteem a boost, you are now a prince, don't you ever forget that. Exercise your rights and authorities over every life`s issues, now you have the authority to do so. You may not attain the highest height with one leap but you will reach your destination if you do not give up.

Do not despise your days of little beginnings. Have faith in that which you are doing and you will achieve much for He who has called you is faithful. Big doors open on small hinges, so don't cast away your confidence. All your battles have been fought and won. You have been declared a winner.

"With your gaze on the Author and Finisher of your
faith, the boisterous wind will go down."
                    -Agu Jaachynma N.E.

Chapter Five

The Prince Offers Help

The whole world lies in darkness, gross darkness. All paupers are groping in the dark and in total confusion. Everyone is doing what he thinks is best but living right is not about doing what you think is best. Rather it is about doing things God`s way, doing what God says is the best! The Prince shows us the right way to follow. He leads us through the right and divine path.

Often times I hear people say, *"I have done everything but nothing seems to be working."* My response to such folks has always been *"you may have done everything you think best but may not have done what God thinks best."* His ways are higher than our ways; His thoughts far more productive than ours. Therefore, the answer we seek lies in doing what He thinks best.

The Prince teaches us via the Holy Spirit and God's words the right things to do; the precepts of the Lord are right and His judgments are sound and true!

How does one get to know the precepts of God? It is by getting connected to the Holy Spirit. He is the greatest Teacher, with Him, the Prince though without formal education taught professors of law - the scribes, the Pharisees and the Sadducees. Though without a medical school certificate, the Prince became the Great Physician.

Without any engineering tutorials, yet He mends broken hearts and homes. He didn't pen any book per se but He is the Author and the Finisher of our faith. All these the Prince did with the help of the Holy Spirit resident in Him

Today, He calls out to anyone willing and obedient saying *"come unto me, all ye that labour and are heavy laden and I will give you rest." (Matthew 11:28)*

The pauper like we have earlier discussed is a labourer, who labours in vain. The pauper from a distance looks pitiable; he is dirty, smelling, with coarse hands that have suffered endlessly. Sweat flows down his face and lines of stress and tiredness are drawn on his forehead. He doesn't respond to greetings, he merely grunts, he does not laugh or smile for that is *"luxury"* for those who have no cares.

He is carrying the weight of his unresolved issues, he is carrying the load of unachieved goals. Heavily burdened with unaccomplished visions and he is pursuing unrealised dreams. He does not even know which comes first; he is just busy doing many things and achieving nothing. His life is completely stressed up; he wakes up early and goes to bed late with nothing accomplished. The following day, he starts again pursuing shadows in place of substances, looking and getting more confused than when he began. Watching him from a distance, one wonders what he is really looking for that he hardly finds. Day in day out he is on the same point, making circles and turning rounds. His life is meaningless, the load is heavy, the journey is long, the path is lonely and dreary. No water to quench his thirst, he has only a dry loaf of bread that he picked up from a garbage can! He is living and swimming in misery! He is pitiable!

As if the physical troubles are not enough, spiritually he is blind, he gropes about in the dark, he is not enlightened for it is the light of God's words that bring enlightenment but the pauper knows neither God nor His Word. His utterances are negative, his heart is filled with fear instead of faith. He is afraid of the next minute, he is uncertain about his future - did you say future? He doesn't know much about that word, all he knows is the now of struggling. He needs help. His physical body is tormented with sores; his mind is overwhelmed with pains. He is confused!

On his head and neck are heavy loads and burdens. He can hardly move; this is one of the reasons why he is only making circles instead of progress. He has no shelter and no hiding place, the rain falls on him, drenching him to his bones, the sun shines on him darkening him and tormenting him the more. The harmattan deals with him making scales off his skin. Look, his legs are fastened with chains, he could hardly walk! There are sores emanating from the reins of the chain. He is beggarly in appearance.

If these were his only problems may be it would have been easier, but his troubles are much more. The mad man by the road sees him coming thinking he is a rival in the realm of madness leashes out on him beating him blue-black! The armed robber thinking he had some treasures in the heavy load he is carrying stops by and when he finds nothing to steal dealt him more blows.

Afflictions upon afflictions, he is indeed helpless and hopeless. Who will rescue him? His kinsmen are waiting for him to pay the money he borrowed from them, his children are expecting him to bring money for their feeding and school fees. His wife is anxiously expecting money for the up-keep of the home. He is confused. He has reached his wit's end; he is tired, he is falling, can someone hold him, offer him a helping hand.

Well, let's see. Someone is coming - No! That's the man he borrowed money from long time ago, he is coming with a whip to add to his troubles. The man leashes out on the pauper, he cries out in pain but there seemed to be no trace of mercy insight. Wait! one of his relatives is coming; he stopped by, looked at him disdainfully, shrugs his shoulders and walks away. Someone else came, spat on him, called him unprintable names and mockingly offered to help him carry his loads. He thought the help was genuine and trying so much to transfer the weight from his head to his *"helper's"* head, he looked up only to discover the "*helper*" has gone, jeering at him.

Come to think of it, which of the loads would he really have given to the man if he was serious - is it the physical one, the emotional trauma, the social, moral, spiritual or financial troubles? Is it his wounded ego? Battered self-image or ruptured future? He sighed for the umpteenth time as tears of pain and grief flow freely down his face!

A friend from his past emerged from no where and offered to take him to where he will be helped. He half crawled and half walked to the place – a religious setting with people like him and a leader who looks like them too.

The pauper swallowed all doubts and decided to give the religious leader some benefits of doubt - "*Bring a white goat, a yellow cock, 21 black candles, a crocodile's eyes and teeth, a lion's tail, a snail's teeth, a purple and white cloth tied together but not touching each other...*" His "*helper's*" voice trailed off reciting items upon items while the pauper's mind wanders off thinking of where to get those things from. As a matter of fact, if he could afford those things or even a quarter of them, then he wouldn't be here for that will mean he has no problems. "*You may go now*", the leader's voice sounded bringing the pauper back to his present predicament. "*But make sure, these items are ready by 12 midnight on the 12th day of the 12th month else your problems will be tripled*", the man concluded.

The pauper came out from that hut more confused, more disappointed, more troubled than he had ever been. His friend encouraged him to go look for those items and walked away leaving him lonelier than he was when his journey began. He slumped down by the wayside and began to mourn his woes. An old school mate appeared and said to him, *"Come, let's go to where your whole troubles will grow wings and fly off"*, he managed to keep pace with his companion as they trudged on again to the sanctuary of the occultists.

"Ah, this is a small case", they told him. He was somehow relieved *"all you need do is bring either your wife or your first son for rituals?"* they told him. Wife? Did they say wife or first son? Of course, they can't be serious these are the people he is struggling for, if he now sacrifices them, who will rejoice and enjoy the wealth with him when it finally comes? Come to think of it, how is he even sure that after the sacrifice, things will turn around for the better? *"No!"* he said feebly. *"It is not possible!"* He begged; they pushed him out of the shrine for they believed he was neither serious nor ready to come out of his distress. The pauper became more troubled than ever, he wanted his life to end so he will be free from it all even if it means going to the hottest part of hell. He preferred anything even if it meant dying a million times better than what he was going through. He got close to a bridge, waited a little, looked left, right and left again to see if anyone was watching so

he could jump into the water and get drowned! He didn't see anyone then he made the first move and looked right again. He saw a piece of crumbled paper and it got his attention because it wasn`t there earlier. He wanted to go ahead with his suicide moves but intuitively decided to give the paper alittle attention. He got down from the cliff and waddled to the paper. He unfolded it, straightened it out and read the contents. What he read made no sense to him initially, he looked again and then it hit him like a thunderbolt… *"Come unto me, all ye that labour and are heavy laden and I will give you rest. Take my yoke upon you, and learn of me; for I am meek and lowly in heart: and ye shall find rest unto your souls. For my yoke is easy, and my burden is light." (Mathew 11: 28-30)*

The pauper kept his gaze on the paper while walking away from the side of the bridge where he earlier went to commit suicide. He finally came to a resting place, sat down and began devouring the contents of the piece of paper again. He read it repeatedly until he almost memorized the whole content. Many questions ran riot in his head, *"who was speaking in this paper? Was the speaker referring to him? Who dropped the piece of paper? Did the person see him trying to commit suicide? Who will explain the contents of this paper to him?"* These and several other questions raced through his mind. Pray! The word dropped on him from nowhere. Pray? How is he supposed to do that? He hasn`t done that before, part of what he read from the paper was an invitation. It said *"come unto me…"* who was making the invitation? He needed a helper out of this quagmire but he didn't know where or who to meet. He has momentarily forgotten his earlier troubles; now he has new ones; however, the later troubles are not as heavy as the former. He preferred the present situation to the previous ones. He clutched the paper to his heart, held it as if solutions will come to him through that paper. Tired, he slept off with the paper still in his hands. He had a fitful sleep, it was as if someone was watching him while he slept but each time he wakes up, he sees nobody. Finally, he got up from where he sat and began pacing the floor, wondering what next to do. Should he go ahead with his earlier suicidal plan or go in search of someone to explain the mysteries contained in this paper to him.

He felt at peace with the second thought but doesn't know where to go for such help. There's no address on the paper but it sounded Christian-like. Maybe he should go to a church, but he was dirty, smelly and covered with sores. He doesn't have good clothings, no, he can't go to a church looking like this. But, he didn't have a better option, maybe he should just go. He has nothing to loose, if they push him out, he will leave. If they welcome him, he will tell them of his predicaments. With his mind made up, he set out in search of a church. He finally arrived at the gate of a church; he stood gaping at it, should he go in or turn back? Just then, a man came out of the magnificent

THE PRINCE & THE PAUPER

building and headed towards him.

The pauper got on his knees and began weeping profusely; the man walked up to him, talked with him at length and made him say the sinner's prayer after which he led him to Christ. The pauper experienced peace within; he knew something good has happened to him for he felt lighter and euphoric. The man smiled at him and led him to a house where he bathed, had a change of clothes and ate good food.

The man introduced himself as a pastor- an anointed servant of the Lord. The pauper narrated his ordeal to the pastor. The Pastor hugged him and made him understand he just had an encounter with the Prince of Peace, the Creator of all things, the One who came to set the captives free. The Alpha and the Omega, the One who has healed his sores and infirmities, the One who has paid all his debts at Calvary. Now! *"You are welcome home,"* the Pastor said hugging him once more. He handed him a black leather book, the pauper opened it and realised it is the complete part of the piece of paper he had. Tears of joy streamed down his cheeks as he realised how much Jesus did for him.

He never knew he was so loved by God all these years and he was living in abject lack, living like a destitute while he`s a prince all along! Now, his woes are over, his pains gone, this is a new him in a new beginning. He is the helped of God! He began studying the word of God, learning more about his new nature, his heritages and his lifestyle. He began praising this God who has dealt so wondrously with him. The Prince of Peace has offered him help, changed his story and enabled him to teach others the way of the Lord. He now has an intimate relationship with the Lord; he lacks nothing good. He has become a voice for the Master telling the untold the message of the gospel. He is no longer a pauper; he is now a prince with God. He is one of the princes whom the Prince of Peace came to transfigure. He now teaches others who they are in Christ, what they have in Christ and the way to enjoy intimacy with the Master of the universe.

***The picture painted above is the author's imagery of a sinner. Does it look familiar to you? The truth is all sinners are in bondage; they are in a state of confusion and lack a sense of direction. This is why we preach the gospel. The gospel means good news. The good news to the poor is that he is now rich, to the sick the good news is perfect healing. Go on and tell someone the good news today. We have paupers around us, we shouldn't keep the good news to ourselves, let's spread it and get more people informed. The gospel is committed to our care, don't let it loose its shine in your hands.*

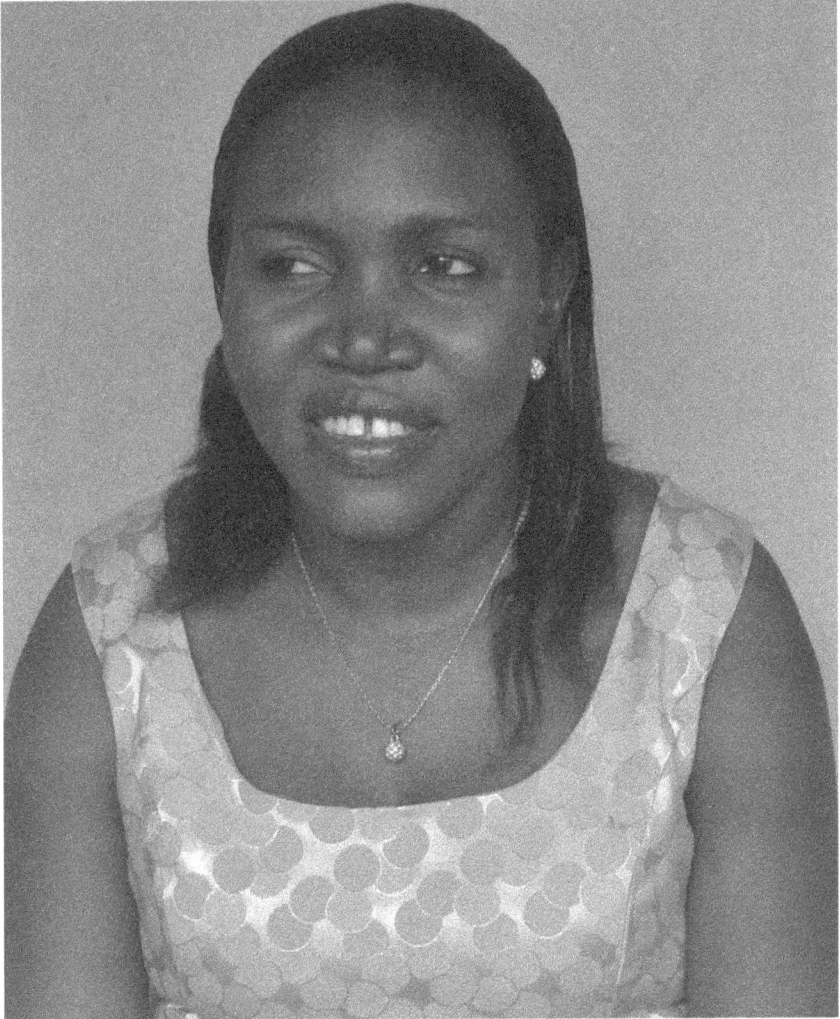

"It doesn`t matter how long and weary Friday seems, Sunday must come."

-Agu Jaachynma N.E.

Chapter Six

The Pathway to Intimacy

No reservoir, regardless of its make or cost, can benefit from any source without a necessary link-up called channel. The source could even be full to overflowing yet it cannot reach the receptacle except there is an established means of conveyance.

Similarly, God is the source of lasting abundance but we being the beneficiaries (*vessels or receptacle*) will get nothing if we don't provide the required means for the flow from Him to us.

Having, therefore, known that God's purpose concerning His people is abundance, it is imperative that we know the channels through which this desired providence could reach us.

This chapter is committed to doing just that. It's a teaching on how-to-be-intimate with the Prince. Now that our personalities have changed, we should know what to do to remain in loving relationship with the Trinity.

In the beginning, before man fell, God had a loving and intimate relationship with man. God loves man so much that He spent the first five days of creation making provisions for the fulfillment of man's desires both physically, emotionally and otherwise.

God comes down in the evenings to chat with man, enjoy man's company and find out how man faired in the course of the day. When satan deceived man, God felt bad. He wanted to still enjoy man's company so He used His Prince- His Only Son as a ransom for man's penalty.

Jesus came not only did He restore man's status, He equally taught man how to live in God's perfect will and presence always. He taught man how to shun off satan whenever the latter rears up his head in man's situation or circumstance. He taught man principles that will keep God and man, in a blissful intimacy! Some of these principles include:

Righteousness…Righteousness is the nature of God; it is having right standing with God. Keeping away from anything that will soil your relationship with God. Righteousness encompasses purity and holiness. **Matthew 5:8** says *"Blessed are the pure in heart, for they shall see God."* It takes a pure heart to see God! **Hebrews 12:14** says: *"… and holiness, without which no one will see the Lord."*

Purity and holiness are like twin brothers, if you are pure in heart you will see God; if you are not holy you will not see God. Jesus taught us all these principles so we don't derail from God's perspective. How does one remain righteous?

Now that your status has changed from being a pauper to

being a prince, you are expected to live the princely life. God expects you to do His word now; you are a product of the word so you must maintain that connection with the word of God.

*Do away with the Babylonian garments…*In the book of **Joshua,** we read the story of how a very small city with a few soldiers defeated the children of Israel in battle. The Israelites became worried, Joshua, their leader knew something was not right; he made enquiries of the Lord and the culprit was brought to limelight.

Joshua 7:1-11: "But the children of Israel committed a trespass in the accursed thing…And the men of Ai smote of them about thirty and six men: for they chased them from before the gate even unto Shebarim, and smote them in the going down: wherefore the hearts of the people melted, and became as water.

And Joshua rent his clothes, and fell to the earth upon his face before the ark of the LORD until the eventide, he and the elders of Israel, and put dust upon their heads…And the LORD said unto Joshua, Get thee up; wherefore liest thou thus upon thy face?... Israel hath sinned, and they have also transgressed my covenant which I commanded them: for they have even taken of the accursed thing…"

The people of Israel made inquiries of the Lord as to why they should be so disgraced by that small city. And God spoke! What did He say?

"Israel has sinned, and they have also transgressed my covenant

which I commanded them. For they have even taken some of the accursed things, and have both stolen and deceived; and they have also put it among their own stuff... Neither will I be with you anymore, unless you destroy the accursed from among you... get up, sanctify the people ... there is an accursed thing in your midst, oh Israel, you cannot stand before your enemies until you take away the accursed thing from among you." (Joshua 7:11-13)

Did you hear that? They sinned, they transgressed! Coveting the accursed things was sin; stealing the accursed things and yet pretending to still be in right standing with God is deception; they transgressed against the Lord`s command.

Achan committed the sin in his closet. Though an Israelite, yet he walked like the heathen. What do you do in your closet? *Those secret dealings in your closet work against you, your family, church, business and career.* They work against your destiny and calling and will infringe on your intimacy with God!

Now that you are born again, what is that charm still doing under your bed? What is the spiritualist still doing in your life? What are those candles, chants and materials from the occult doing around you? Why are you still working in hatred and keeping malice? Now that you are born again, do away with those *sugar-daddies and gigolos. "The Lord has no delight in fools" (Ecclesiastes 5:4).*

If you are for God, stand for Him, if you are on the other side then don't pretend move over to the camp of the enemy. There is no sitting on the fence in spiritual matters; you are either for light or for darkness.

Do away with all those Babylonian garments and foods; you don`t need them, if you do the Lord is faithful and rich enough to supply all your needs. Don`t cut corners! Whatever the Lord didn`t give you is not worth having. Learn to take the right decisions and stand by them. You can refuse to append your mandate to those illegal documents; refuse to do that wrong thing which every other person is doing.

I know of a young medical doctor, who went for a job interview in a renowned hospital, after the interview, it was obvious the job was his judging from his performance and the comments from the interview panel. Then one of the panelists quickly told him the hospital specializes in termination of unwanted pregnancies especially for young unmarried women. The young doctor told them he is a Christian and wouldn`t get involved with such practice. They told him he would hear from them, of course, he never did. Learn to stand by what you profess, that a million others are doing the wrong thing doesn't make that wrong act right. *Read more on these from my book titled:* **RISK IT, BE DIFFERENT!**

You can do it. It's not difficult to say "*No*" to the advances of those married men; say "*No*" to the lures of those married women. You can say "*No*" to the devil and mean No!

God doesn't abandon you when you stand out for him. When Joshua and the people of Israel detected the defaulter and dealt with him accordingly, God was happy with them, He returned to their camp and granted them more victories: **Joshua 8:24-25** says: "*...when Israel had made an end of slaying all the inhabitants of Ai...so it was that all who fell that day, both men and women, were twelve thousand —even all the men of Ai.*"

At another occasion, the children of Israel strayed from the Lord's command, this time they were sleeping with prostitutes from an unbelieving nation. God was angry with them and wanted to destroy their leaders but a young man called Phinehas stood in the gap. He maintained his right standing with God and the plague that had already visited the land, was averted by this man's act of righteousness...**Numbers 25:1-12**, "*And Israel abode in Shittim, and the people began to commit whoredom with the daughters of Moab... Israel joined himself unto Baalpeor: and the anger of the LORD was kindled against Israel. And the LORD said unto Moses, Take all the heads of the people, and hang them up before the LORD against the sun, that the fierce anger of the LORD may be turned away from Israel. And Moses said unto the* *judges of Israel, Slay ye every one his men that were joined unto Baalpeor. And, behold, one of the children of Israel came and brought unto his brethren a Midianitish woman in the sight of Moses, and in the sight of all the congregation of the children of Israel, who were weeping before the door of the tabernacle of the congregation. And when Phinehas, the son of Eleazar, the son of Aaron the priest, saw it, he rose up from among the congregation, and took a javelin in his hand; And he went after the man of Israel into the tent, and thrust both of them through, the man of Israel, and the woman through her belly. So the plague was stayed from the children of Israel"*

Hear what God said about Phinehas: *"Phinehas the son of Eleazar, the son of Aaron the Priest, had turned back my wrath from the Children of Israel, because he was zealous with my zeal among them, so that I did not consume the children of Israel in my zeal. Therefore say, "Behold, I give to him my covenant of Peace…"* **(Numbers 25:11-12).**

Your decision to stand separate from the crowd will enhance your vision, it will grant you access into the revelation of how to deliver your family, your country, business, profession or even your church! Stand separate and do God`s word, there is reward in doing His word. It may interest you to know that in the Old Testament, they were called to obey God`s commandments but in the New Testament we are called to *DO* His Word.

Job 36:11 says: *"If they obey and serve Him they shall spend their days in prosperity, and their years in pleasure!"*

God rewards every act of obedience to His willl. That everyone is doing it doesn't change God's standard. Dare to be different. Represent your Maker well and you will forever abide in the beautiful embrace of His loving arms and enjoy intimate moments with him!

Remaining in His Presence... Remaining in His is another principle you require to have intimacy with God.

God's presence is very vital to believers. There is abundance of all you need to make your life comfortable in His presence. His presence is everywhere but His manifested presence is not everywhere. **Psalm 16:11** says: *"You will show me the path of life; in your presence is fullness of joy, at your right hand are pleasures forevermore."*

Until you become conversant with His presence, you will not experience His fullness of joy and pleasures forever more. His presence brings the unction to function in your life, career, church, etc. His presence makes the difference.

Moses knew the importance of His presence that is why he said: *"... if your presence does not go with us, do not bring us up from here"* *(Exodus 33:15).* The presence of the Lord terminates all kinds of life's struggles. His presence makes alive, His presence brings goodness and unending prosperity. His presence makes whole. His presence brings power and boldness, there is no place like His presence!

The whole of **Psalm 23** talks about the presence of the Lord: *"...I will fear no evil; For You are with me; Your rod and Your staff they comfort me..."* **(Psalm 23:4)**.

There is fullness of joy in His presence. Sin cannot have dominion over you when you dwell in God`s presence, you stay pure and holy. His presence causes the righteous to experience peace while making the wicked tremble. The Psalmist said in **Psalms 114: 7-8:** *"Tremble, O earth, at the presence of the Lord, at the presence of the God of Jacob who turned the rock into a pool of water, the flint into a fountain of waters."*

Jesus never left God`s presence while here on earth that`s why He completely fulfilled His purpose. Joseph was always in this Divine presence, no wonder the devil couldn`t halt his journey to the Egyptian palace despite all hurdles. Daniel, even in the Lion's den carried the presence of God, hence his ability to use the lions as pillows! It sure takes the presence of God to do that! Moses had His presence; all the elders of old who walked distinctly with the Lord never left His presence.

When you are in His presence, favour answers to you at all times. In His presence there is no tiredness or weariness rather you find His strength and ability to help you out in times of need. When you encounter His presence, your knowledge of Him will increase and your foundations will not be shaken. In His presence, you experience His glory and remain revived always! You encounter His words that bring light to your path. Get to His presence, remain there and activate His power to work for you and through you.

The third principle in maintaining intimacy with God is:

Worship…Worship is an intimate union of two Spirits - the Spirit of God and that of man. During worship, you show your adoration, admiration, respect and devotion to God. Man most of the times is busy chasing too many things and relegating God to the background. You cannot go far in life when you live independent of God. Worship comes handy when you want to express your feelings and thoughts to God. He is like your spouse so treat and relate with Him as such. He is your True Friend, Lover, King, Loving Father etc.

At worship, you shower praises to God, you minster to Him and appreciate Him. You shower Him with the genuine and true love He deposited in your heart. It is interesting to know that He sought us out first, God loved us first and called us to live the best life in the Kingdom of His dear Son.

Your time of worship to God shouldn't be spontaneous rather it should be planned. Have a set time when you worship God, minister to Him and give Him attention.

Don't do it because you feel like it, do it because you know you love Him and should worship Him. *"God is a Spirit: and they that worship him must worship him in spirit and in truth"* (*John 4:24*).

Count your blessings and name them one by one. *An Attitude of Gratitude Delivers to You the Altitude of Beatitudes.* Remember the ten lepers that Jesus cleansed, only one came back to worship and give thanks and his healing and cleansing were perfected.

Luke 17:14-15 *"... And it came to pass, that, as they went, they were cleansed. And one of them, when he saw that he was healed, turned back, and with a loud voice glorified God,"*

The queue for people seeking blessings is usually longer than that of those coming to give thanks to God. It shouldn't be that way. Be as enthusiastic to worship and thank God as you were when seeking for that miracle. Remember, if you don't appreciate, you depreciate; begin to give God praise and worship. Adore Him for all He is and all He has done for you! Truly, He deserves it.

The fourth principle in maintaining intimacy with God is:

Confession... Confession is speaking the same thing with God. Your words should be in agreement with God not at variance. Your spoken words are important in your relationship with God; they confirm that you accept what

God has said concerning you. Your mouth is not given to you for feeding alone; it is given to you to programme events and circumstances around you to suit your purpose. You recreate your world to your taste with God's word in your mouth.

Your words are powerful, what you say goes a long way to either establish or destroy you. Therefore, say things that God has said concerning you and not what situations say. Do not be defined by your circumstance rather be defined by God's word. God created the world with His words – He spoke therefore you should speak as well.

If you check **Mark 11:23**, you will discover that the word SAY was used four times while the word BELIEVE was used once! *"For verily I **say** unto you, That whosoever shall **say** unto this mountain, Be thou removed, and be thou cast into the sea; and shall not doubt in his heart, but shall believe that those things which he **saith** shall come to pass; he shall have whatsoever he **saith**".*

The key to change that situation is in your mouth, believe it and say it. What you say concerning your life, family, marriage, children, career, nation and ministry matters a lot. Besides, the devil cannot read your mind; he doesn't have that power he only acts on what he hears you say. When pressure is on, watch your words for God is listening and the devil is listening too. What will God hear?

Things that will make Him proud of you or things that will make His shoulders drop. What will the devil hear? Things that will send him running away from you in utter defeat and shame or things that will make him feel triumphant over God? Watch your words!

The choice is yours. Don't let your pronouncements destroy your destiny rather let them build your future! Don't say negative things about your spouse and children. Recreate your world with God's Word in your mouth; just say it and have what you say!

In **Romans 10:9**, the Bible says: *"that if you confess with your mouth the Lord Jesus and believe in your heart that God raised Him from the dead you will be saved."*

Salvation is all about confession! Talk yourself up the ladder of success. Salvation is all encompassing, it is not just about being saved from sin, it includes being saved from other negative influences and circumstances too. Enjoy your salvation package to the full by speaking words of power.

Let your words glorify God, edify your hearers and beautify your life. Words are directed to four personalities namely: God, your hearers, devil and yourself. Weigh whatever you are about to say; what will it bring to God - honour, glory or embarrassment? What will it do to your hearer - encouragement, edification, disappointment or fear? What will it do to the devil - power to dominate you or make him flee from you? What will it do to your life - glorify, edify, beautify or weigh you down? Speak well and things will go well!

Meditation... This is another principle that will perfect your intimacy with God. Meditation is like rumination, where you regurgitate food and chew it over again. In mediation, you go over a particular thought or word repeatedly. You dwell on the said information, think deeply about it, mutter it repeatedly to yourself so it will register and finally shout it out to drown the other voices or negative information around you.

As a child of God, you have the Spirit of God resident in you, you relate with Him through meditation and speaking in tongues. When you meditate on the word and mutter it to yourself, you activate the power behind the word. Meditation is a vital tool in building an intimacy with the Lord. Employ it today and watch your life soar!

"Your decision to stand separate from the crowd will enhance your vision and grant you access into deeper revelations!"

~ Agu, Jaachynma N.E.

Chapter Seven

Exchange of Positions

The Father has delivered us out of satan's control and dominion. This He did through the vicarious death and victorious resurrection of Christ Jesus. He has brought us home to where we belong. We should live by the godly standard and abide by the principles of our loving Father; our assessing His blessings is dependent on our doing His word.

When man fell, the devil took man's position and began acting with man's authority. God instructed man at creation to rule, reign and have dominion. However, at the fall of man, the devil became the god of this world wielding the authority that once belonged to man.

Man was under the influence of the devil, subjected to afflictions of all sorts until Christ came. When Jesus arrived the scene, the devil didn't realise the game was up for him. He even came to Christ asking Him to bow down to him in order to get back the authority that man threw away. Jesus hushed him off with the Word of God; at the appointed time, Jesus dealt with him. He rendered him powerless, made an open show of him, collected from him man's authority as well as the keys of death and hell!

Jesus gave man the authority over satan and all things:

"And Jesus came and spake unto them, saying, All power is given unto me in heaven and in earth" **(Mathew 28: 18)**...*"Behold, I give unto you power to tread on serpents and scorpions, and over all the power of the enemy: and nothing shall by any means hurt you"* (**Luke 10:19**).

Man is no longer under the influence of the devil, man now rules over all things, devil inclusive. The Prince of Peace took the place of the pauper and died for the pauper to be free. The pauper is now a prince with God, his status has changed, Jesus has paid his debt, Halleluiah!

Jesus was killed for the sins He did not commit. He was killed outside the city just like a lamb that was used for atonement of sin in the days of Aaron the priest. He bore all the pains, shame and torture on our account. He took upon Himself everything that we ought to suffer so we won't go through them anymore. He was sinless but became sin for us.

Jesus collected the keys from satan and freed man from all torments. He set man free from all sins, bondages and curses of life. He gave man a new nature; He bestowed glory, honour, beauty, power, dominion and eternal life on man. He used His life to pay for man's debts!

The Bible says, *"Christ redeemed us from that self-defeating, cursed life by absorbing it completely into himself. Do you remember the Scripture that says, "Cursed is everyone who hangs on a tree"?*

That is what happened when Jesus was nailed to the Cross: He became a curse, and at the same time dissolved the curse." **(Galatians 3:13 MSG)** Christ redeemed us from all the curses of the law. We are therefore advised to thank God for this great plan of redemption, which He planned and sent His Prince to carry out.

Jesus didn't take your position because you can pray well, neither is it because of the fat offerings you give. It was done out of God`s love for man! He is not asking you to pay Him back, He's only saying hand your life over to God who is capable of handling all your problems. He says, *"if you do what I say, you will enjoy what I have."*

All who acknowledged what Grace did for them on Calvary, have stepped into a higher realm in all aspects of life. Now, they are above only!

The **Book of Deuteronomy 28 :1, 2 & 13** says: *"And it shall come to pass, if thou shalt hearken diligently unto the voice of the Lord thy God to observe and to do all His commandments which I command thee this day, that the Lord thy God will set thee on high* above all *nations of the earth. And all these blessings shall come on thee and overtake thee, if thou shalt hearken unto the voice of the Lord thy God. And the Lord shall make thee the head, and not the tail, and thou shall be* above only, *and thou shalt not be beneath, if thou hearken unto the commandments of the Lord thy God, which I command thee this day, to observe and to do them."*

Being above only is not for everyone, it's only for those who acknowledge the pain Jesus underwent for their glory. It is for those who recognized Jesus' sweat is for their sweet and appreciate the Prince's death to give them life.

Jesus wants man to be an all-round success like their Father in Heaven. He wants man to live and enjoy eternal life that is why He took man's position and bore his pains. He bore the punishments and consequences of man's actions!

This is the gospel. It is worth shouting about, unfortunately, many believers are silent about it. They prefer to be silent Christians but the blessings of God are for the bold and courageous. It's for those who can stand up to anything to defend the Name of the Lord. Telling the untold about the vicarious death of Christ on the cross doesn't bring you down rather it takes you up.

No wonder there are several vacancies on top. Most people prefer to stay down out of ignorance; they want to be quiet Christians, how sad! What Christ did for humanity at Calvary shouldn't be taken lightly at all. We shouldn't call vain the pains He went through! We should tell our world the news and turn them to Christ. Jesus loves us more than we can even love ourselves.

While on earth, He assumed man's position in all things. He was born in a manger amidst animals while man stayed in luxurious suites. During His years of ministry on earth, man always intruded into His comfort, privacy and time; He will forgo His own needs and meet man`s needs.

He had to wake up early in order to enjoy communion with His Father as He wouldn`t have time in the day when man is awake. He wouldn`t want to leave man all by himself while having a time of fellowship with His Father!

He blessed bread and fed man while He went hungry, He trekked on the sea while His disciples (*Man*) enjoyed their trip in a ship! His focus was to make man comfortable. Man stole, Jesus was punished for the stealing. Man lied; Jesus answered a liar and a blasphemous being. He was flogged for man to be healed.

He received a crown of thorns for man to wear a crown of glory. They took His garment and left Him naked for man to be clothed. He died for man to live! What's His crime? His crime is that He loves man and wants man to be comfortable!

The Prince is above all powers and every created thing. He is above all the ways of men, He was here before the world began, nothing can express or measure His worth! Yet, He left all of that took the place of man and died a shameful death for man to live. God- the Father turned His face away from Jesus- the Son because the later was sin personified and the former does not behold iniquity.

At this point, the Prince became lonely and filled with so much pains; He cried with a loud voice. He wailed, He groaned, His agony was visible, He couldn't hold it anymore, He cried out: *"Eloi, Eloi, lama sabachthani?"* meaning *"My God, my God, why have you forsaken me?"* (**Mark 16:34**). He spoke to the Father in another tongue, He was broken with the weight of man`s sins, challenges, unfulfilled dreams etc.

He bore the pains and iniquities of all humanity. He suffered and died for man to live a stress-free life. Jesus changed His status for man's sake; His name was altered, His glory smeared because of man. Will you take this sacrifice for granted?

As I end this chapter, I want you to envision Jesus saying the following words to you: *"I shed my blood and gave my life for you so you will be cleansed and have eternal life; what will you do for me? I gave my years, my time, my peace; I was flogged, beaten and I wept, just to give you comfort, health and the good life. I did all these and more for you, what have you done for me?*

To save you, I had to leave my Father's throne and all kingly services: respect and honour accrued to me; I was disgraced so you will be honoured, I did all these for you, what are you doing for me"?

The most important question for all humanity is "What are you doing for the Master?"

"Every pauper has a battered self-image, a wounded ego and a ruptured future, yet, he can live a princely life and be a leading light by simply connecting to the Prince of Peace."

- Agu Jaachynma N.E.

Chapter Eight

The Pauper-Turned-Prince

The status of the pauper has changed. His name, yes, his identity has changed! He is now a new creation, whose origin is of God, he hails from God now. Spiritually, his origin is no longer traceable to his biological family. He is now a child of God; Jesus has become his elder brother. He has the same genotype with Christ, the same blood group, the same hemoglobin that the Father has! Jesus is indestructible and so is the pauper now! None can curse Jesus and none can curse the pauper too. He is now a prince with God; God lavished so much love on him. Now, He is not ashamed to call him son!

1ˢᵗ John 3:1, *"Behold what manner of love the Father has bestowed upon us, that we should be called children of God!*

Being a son of God has benefits and rights, the whole creation now looks up to the pauper-turned-prince. **Romans 8:19** says, *"For the earnest expectation of creation eagerly waits for the revealing of the sons of God"* His adoption into the Fatherhood of God is by faith in Jesus and His saving power.

Galatians 3:26, *"...for you are all sons of God through faith in Christ Jesus"* Now, the pauper-turned-prince is in power. Things that happen to other paupers won`t happen to him because his story has changed. Transformation has taken place within him.

1st Peter 2:9-10 (NKJV) describes him better, *"But you are a chosen generation, a royal priesthood, a holy nation, His own special people, that you may proclaim the praises of Him who called you out of darkness into His marvellous light. Who once were not a people but are now THE PEOPLE OF GOD! Who had not obtained mercy, but now have obtained mercy"*

Jesus describing the pauper-turned- prince in **John 15:14-16** said: *"You are my friends ... no longer do I call you servants for a servant does not know what his master is doing; but I have called you friends for all things that I heard from my Father I have made known to you. You did not choose me but I chose you ..."*

While praying for the pauper-turned-prince in **John 17:9-10**, Jesus made the following declarations: *"I pray for them. I do not pray for the world but for those whom you have given me, for they are yours. And all mine are yours, and yours are mine and I am glorified in them".*

Jesus referred to the paupers-turned-princes as friends! He didn't refer to them as servants or little ones but friends. They have become friends with Jesus.

The psalmist in **Psalms 82:6** speaking God`s mind declares, *"Ye are Gods and all of you are the children of the Most High"* If you are born again, your position has changed. You are a new creature, your old nature is passed away, every old thing about you is gone, and everything is made new and perfect!

You now bear in your body the mark of our Lord Jesus Christ. His Names have become yours! Your declarations made in His Name receive heaven's attention. Everything about you has God's stamp on it! **Colossians 3:17** opines *"And whatsoever ye do in word or indeed, do all in the Name of the Lord Jesus, giving thanks to God the Father by Him"*

The encounter with the King of kings made you divine. You have dropped your old name and status as a pauper. Now, you are reigning with the Master. This same encounter made you a joint – heir with Christ. It brought you into partnership with Him. You now have a relationship, a union with Him. Whatever belongs to Him belongs to you as well.

You have given yourself in commitment to God and God has given himself to you in total commitment too. When you are in this kind of relationship, you are no longer your own property! Your assets, debts, strengths, weaknesses are turned to Him and He sure knows how to turn your sweat into sweet.

When you think of the marriage relationship between a man and his wife and you will understand this more! When you are in a marriage relationship with someone, that person's name becomes yours! Likewise, when you unite with Christ in salvation, His Name becomes yours to use.

When you received Jesus as your Lord and Saviour, He took your name and you took His! Your names were sin, weakness, fear, poverty, failure, death and other evil things you inherited from the first Adam. Jesus took those names and nailed them on the Cross and gave you His own Names in exchange!

Ephesians 3:14-15 reiterates: *"For this reason I bow my knees to the Father of our Lord Jesus Christ, from whom the whole family in heaven and earth is named!"*

The family here refers to the Body of Christ; the Believers in heaven and on earth have been named after Christ. This means you have been given Jesus' Name. The power, respect, honour and authority associated with His Name is yours because you are now a prince like Him! You are now a member of His family; you belong to the class of Gods now!

You are no longer permitted to suffer what others suffer, you can no longer fail or die prematurely. You will no more live and die as a non-entity because you have encountered the greatness that is associated with Christ and His Name!

The Prince you have identified with has the following as some of His Names and descriptions:

- **Prince and Saviour**: *"Him hath God exalted with his right hand to be a Prince and a Saviour..."* (**Acts 5:31**)

- **Prince of Life**: *"...the Prince of life, whom God hath raised from the dead..."* (**Acts 3:15**)

- **Prince of the Kings of the Earth**: *"And from Jesus Christ...the prince of the kings of the earth..."* (**Revelation 1:5**)

- **Prince of Peace**: *"For unto us a child is born...The Prince of Peace"* (**Isaiah 9:6**)

- **Jesus**: *"And she shall bring forth a son, and thou shalt call his name JESUS: for he shall save..."* (**Matthew 1:21**)

- **Mighty God:** *"For unto us a child is born and his name shall be called ...The mighty God..."* (**Isaiah 9:6**)

- **Wisdom of God**: *"...Christ the power of God, and the wisdom of God"* (**1 Corinthians 1:24**)

- **Deliverer**: *"...as it is written, There shall come out of Sion the Deliverer..."* (**Romans 11:26**)

- **The Lion of the Tribe of Judah**: *"...behold, the Lion of the tribe of Juda...prevailed..."* (**Revelation 5:5**)

- **Word of Life**: *"That which was from the beginning, which we have heard, which we have seen with our eyes...the Word of life"* (**1 John 1:1**)

- **Word of God**: *"For the word of God is quick, and powerful, and sharper than any two-edged sword..."* (**Hebrews 4:12**)

- **Advocate**: *"My little children, these things write I unto you, that ye sin not. And if any man sin, we have an advocate with the Father, Jesus Christ the righteous:"* (**1 John 2:1**)

- **Provider**: *"But my God shall supply all your need according to his riches in glory by Christ Jesus"* (**Philippians 4:19**)

- **Helper**: *"...The Lord is my helper, and I will not fear what man shall do unto me"* (**Hebrews 13:6**)

- **Healer:** *"But he was wounded for our transgressions, he was bruised for our iniquities: the chastisement of our peace was upon him; and with his stripes we are healed"* (**Isaiah 53:5**)

- **Emmanuel**: *"... and they shall call his name Emmanuel, which being interpreted is, God with us"* (**Matthew 1:23**)

- **Wonderful Counselor, The Everlasting Father**: *"...and his name shall be called Wonderful Counsellor...The everlasting Father..."* (**Isaiah 9:6**)

- **Lamb of God**: *"...Behold the Lamb of God, which taketh away the sin of the world"* (**John 1:29**)

- **Lord of Hosts**: *"... the LORD of hosts is his name..."* (**Isaiah 54:5**)

- **Root of David**: *"... the Root of David, hath prevailed to open the book, and to loose the seven seals thereof"* (**Revelation 5:5**)

- **Author and Finisher of Our Faith**: *"Looking unto Jesus the author and finisher of our faith..."*(**Hebrews 12:2**)

- **The Way, The Truth The Life**: *"Jesus saith unto him, I am the way, the truth and the life..."* (**John 14:6**)

- **Son of God**: *"...Of a truth thou art the Son of God"* (**Matthew 14:33**)

- **Chief Cornerstone**: *"...Jesus Christ himself being the chief corner stone;"* (**Ephesians 2:20**)

- **King of Kings**: *"...for he is...King of kings..."* (**Revelation 17:14**)

- **Lord of All**: *"… he is Lord of all"* (**Acts 10:36**)

- **The Light of the World**: *"…I am the light of the world: he that followeth me shall not walk in darkness, but shall have the light of life."* (**John 8:12**)

- **Great Shepherd**: *"… that great shepherd of the sheep…"* (**Hebrews 13:20**)

- **Righteous Judge**: *"Henceforth there is laid up for me a crown of righteousness, which the Lord, the righteous judge, shall give me at that day: …"* (**2 Timothy 4:8**)

- **Sun of Righteousness**: *"But unto you that fear my name shall the Sun of righteousness arise with healing in his wings; …"* (**Malachi 4:2**)

- **The Resurrection and life**: *"… I am the resurrection, and the life: …"* (**John 11:25**)

- **The Alpha and the Omega**: *"I am Alpha and Omega, the beginning and the ending… I am Alpha and Omega, the first and the last:…"* (**Revelation 1:8,11**)

Friend, you have been given all these names amongst others and they cover all your needs - every need you will ever have is met because you agreed to follow the Prince home! The Power of God is on all these Names and makes every knee or need in your life bow to the Name of

Jesus! Hallelujah.

Philippians 2:9-11 says: *"Therefore, God has highly exalted Him and given Him the Name which is above every other name, that at the Name of Jesus every knee should bow, of things in heaven, and of things on earth and of things beneath the earth, and that every tongue should confess that Jesus Christ is Lord, to the glory of God the Father."*

Don't be overwhelmed by the enormity of your trials or number of the challenges. They only came to make your testimony more beautiful. *"Many are the afflictions of the righteous but the Lord delivers him out of them all. He guards all his bones, and not one of them is broken"* **Psalm 34:19-20***:* You have changed, you are now a Prince, think it, talk it, walk it and act it!

Paul, writing to Titus reminded him not to allow any situation or any one put him down. Titus was to remember who he was. **Titus 2:15**, *"Speak these things, exhort and rebuke with all authority. Let no one despise you!"*

Don't allow any situation intimidate you, don't accept defeat anymore. Your names have changed so has your up-look and outlook! Don't call yourself discouraged anymore; it's no longer your name. When the devil yells *"Hey, poor fellow!"* Don't look back because it's not your name. Jesus has taken those old names away from you forever. They are gone for good! Keep meditating on the new names the Lord has bestowed on you.

All of these names mentioned above are wrapped up in the name of Jesus, the Name above all names. You now have this Name with all its powers and attributes. You are on top, remain there! Move ahead in life, leave behind the former things. You are now a brand new man!

Be a king. Dare to be different, dare to manifest. Be a pioneer, a pace setter, a leader in your career. Be the kind of person who in the face of adversity will continue to embrace life and walk fearlessly towards the challenge. Be a man who is bold. Be a Prince whom people will look up to at all times. Be brave! Be a truth seeker and reign over all in your Kingdom. Your kingdom may be your home, your office, your career, your community, your church, family or profession. Reign in these domains with a large heart filled with liquid love, trust and compassion for all, your Maker inclusive!

Be a king. Be a ruler. Be strong. Continue to father new ideas for your family, community, church, business and profession. Use the new Name you now have to the full. Always rejoice in the strength of your manliness in God. My prayer is for you to stop wasting time on trivial things that are too tiny to stop you. Go in hot pursuit of your purpose! You can do all things. Remember you are like Jesus. Jesus, your friend and brother was a worker. In this new family, there is no room for laxity, Abraham worked, and so did Isaac and Jacob. God worked for 24 hours in six days non-stop! You are a child of God here on earth to teach the world how to live! *Don't fizzle out without fulfilling your purpose.*

It doesn't matter what you've been through, where you came from, who your parents are, or your academic, social and economic status. None of these count; you have been changed! You have received a new name. How do you choose to live? How do you want to reign? What plans are you making to dominate your Kingdom? How do you intend to express your superiority over events and times? How do you choose to present to the world what's on the inside of you? How do you choose to train those in your loins right now? These are the things that count. Your answers to these questions will show whether you are still bearing your old name or you have taken over the new one completely!

Be the king that Christ has crowned you; reign in your own power, will and glory! Dominate in your domain. You can do it. Jesus did it so you can!

All that Jesus did, He did for you; He loves you so much and wants the best of everything for you. He gave His all so you can enjoy all things. He gave His life for you to have yours. He didn't do all He did because we are many;

He did it because He loves us individually. We worth so much to Him, we are very valuable to Him.

The Bible says in **Matthew 18:12-14**, *"...Even so it is not the will of Your Father who is in heaven that one of these little ones should perish."* He came out of His Father's bosom and took the form of a man, His mission on earth was reconciling man to God-His Father. He taught man the benefits of being His Father's children. When man accepted His teachings and way of life, He took man home to His Father and man became His sibling!

Before the Prince left the earth back to heaven, He prayed a prayer of love to His Father on behalf of the other princes. **John 17:6-19**, *"I have manifested thy name unto the men which thou gavest me out of the world: thine they were, and thou gavest them me; and they have kept thy word. Now they have known that all things whatsoever thou hast given me are of thee. For I have given unto them the words which thou gavest me; and they have received them, and have known surely that I came out from thee, and they have believed that thou didst send me. I pray for them: I pray not for the world, but for them which thou hast given me; for they are thine. And all mine are thine, and thine are mine; and I am glorified in them. And now I am no more in the world, but these are in the world, and I come to thee. Holy Father, keep through thine own name those whom thou hast given me, that they may be one, as we are. While I was with them in the world, I kept them in thy name: those that thou gavest me I have kept, and none of them is* *lost, but the son of perdition; that the scripture might be fulfilled. And now come I to thee; and these things I speak in the world, that they might have my joy fulfilled in themselves. I have given them thy word; and the world hath hated them, because they are not of the world, even as I am not of the world. I pray not that thou shouldest take them out of the world, but that thou shouldest keep them from the evil. They are not of the world, even as I am not of the world. Sanctify them through thy truth: thy word is truth. As thou hast sent me into the world, even so have I also sent them into the world. And for their sakes I sanctify myself, that they also might be sanctified through the truth."*

Jesus cares, He loves us, He really wants the best for us! Jesus prayed for us! We may not have gone to heaven to see His Father and our Father, His God and our God but we know Him spiritually and He knows us as well. Jesus said to His disciples: *"Where I am going you know and the way you know as well." (**John 14:4**).* He asked the Father to send us the Holy Spirit who will guide us into all truth now we have link, access into His will and plans through the Holy Spirit. We all work together – the Prince in heaven, who is the Heir apparent to the throne and the princes here on earth who are joint-heirs with Him plus the Holy Spirit who connects us to Christ. Christ is up in heaven with the Father but always with us, around us and within us in the Person of the Holy Spirit.

There is really no difference between Him and us. For the scripture says, *"Love has been perfected among us in this: that we may have boldness in the Day of Judgment; because* **as He is, so are we in this world."** *(1st John 4:17)*

We are His exact replicas, the same blood that is divine, that speaks better things than the blood of Abel is the same blood that flows in our arteries and veins and that is why sickness cannot harm us. Life will be a whole lot better if we understand what our salvation in Christ means. This is why we shouldn`t focus on defeating the devil for our elder brother – Jesus Christ, has defeated him for us.

We are identified with the one who has victory over death and satan. We are identified with the Risen Lord of lords, the Mighty God, the one that conquered death and all diseases on the cross. We are identified with the Risen Christ! With this, diseases have no hold on us!

The Father loves us as much as He loves Him. We are princes like Him, we are not any less powerful or Spirit filled than He is, because He gave us ALL powers that were accorded to Him when He defeated death on the Cross. **Matthew 28:18-20**, *"And Jesus came and spake unto them, saying, All power is given unto me in heaven and in earth. Go ye therefore, and teach all nations, baptizing them in the name of the Father, and of the Son, and of the Holy Ghost: Teaching them to* *observe all things whatsoever I have commanded you: and, lo, I am with you alway, even unto the end of the world. Amen."*

Jesus sees us as having all it takes to succeed for He gave us the glory His Father gave Him. **John 17:22-23***:"And the glory which thou gavest me I have given them; that they may be one, even as we are one: I in them, and thou in me, that they may be made perfect in one; and that the world may know that thou hast sent me, and hast loved them, as thou hast loved me."*

It's a pity that most of us don't understand fully what we have in Christ. The testimonies of people who know their place in Christ and are maximizing it to the full thrills me.

This testimony of a man of God called John G. Lake is one of such… *"An epidemic broke out in one part of Africa where John G. Lake was residing as an Evangelist. It was a very contagious disease that only touching of the patients gets one infected. But this man of God was on daily basis making contacts with the patients as he assists in nursing them. This he did without being infected. When asked how that was possible, he told them he had a different life at work in him and that if any disease or germ got in touch with his body, they would die, by the reason of the Life that's at work in him! When asked to prove it, he agreed to a test. Samples of these germs that affected many inhabitants of that land were collected and dropped in John G. Lake's hand.*

They viewed the germ cells with a microscope to be sure those germs were still alive when placed on John G. Lake's hand. After

134

sometime, the scientists checked the germs on the Evangelist's hand again with the microscope and discovered they have all died! They were no longer moving like before!"

Do these scientists need any more preaching? Of course, the good news had already been shared; principalities and powers have been disgraced. No wonder the Bible says concerning Christ in **Colossians 2:15**, *"And having spoiled principalities and powers, he made a shew of them openly, triumphing over them in it."*

The powers of sufferings, infirmities, lack, and every other power of the enemy have been paralysed by Jesus Christ! Jesus paralysed satan and all his cohorts through His death on the cross. The scripture says in **Hebrews 2:14**, *"...that through death He might destroy him who had the power of death, that is, the devil."* He destroyed both death and the one who had the dominion of death. He overthrew the hosts of demons and satan himself!

The beautiful thing about this conquest is that Jesus didn't do it for Himself; He doesn't need the power, victory et al. He is already the only Son of God and so lacked nothing! He could have preferred to sit back with his Father on His throne and enjoy all the luxuries accorded him as *un fils unique* of a very wealthy and powerful lineage!

But, He said No! He looked at man's pitiable state. He saw the devil dealing hard blows of hunger, deprivation - yes, the devil imprisoned man and deprived him of his basic spiritual rights. Jesus looked and saw the weight of cares, uncertainties and weariness that man was carrying, and accepted to die for man`s freedom!

Jesus could have preferred to make flowers and lilies His friends and companions since they have no problems and have no burdens, *"And why take ye thought for raiment? Consider the lilies of the field, how they grow; they toil not, neither do they spin: And yet I say unto you, That even Solomon in all his glory was not arrayed like one of these."* (**Matthew 6:28, 29**)

He could have picked on the birds that will not cause Him pain for their redemption. He had a choice for He is the only son of the Omnipotent and Omniscient God, *"Who, being in the form of God, thought it not robbery to be equal with God: But made himself of no reputation, and took upon him the form of a servant, and was made in the likeness of men: And being found in fashion as a man, he humbled himself, and became obedient unto death, even the death of the cross."* (***Philippians 2:6-8***).

He saw other options but chose to liberate man who is made in the image and likeness of God. What more, He has not only made us princes with Him, He equally has taken us and introduced us to His Father so we could be partakers of the divine life. He shared with us ALL the glory He received from His Father. Christ is in love with us, He is actually crazy about us.

With this, infirmities and afflictions shouldn't dominate us anymore. He has paid all the debt we owed; we shouldn't allow our ex-creditors - devil and his cohorts to harass us anymore. We are no longer indebted to them; our freedom has been paid for, we should therefore walk out on satan into our freedom! We are now princes, heirs unto God and joint-Heirs with Christ. Jesus Himself called us His friends, can you beat that? The only Son of the Creator of all things, the Only Son of the Mighty God, the Sole Heir to an empire of inestimable value introduce us to people and the host of heavens as His friends! **John 15:14-16**, *"Ye are my friends..."*

Imagine the son of an Head of State or a Governor's son introducing you to people as his close friend and telling them you didn't choose him but he chose you. I am sure you will feel a lot taller than you really are. Now, think of Jesus Christ introducing you to the Host of Heaven as His one and only friend. Remember, He is the Son of the living God, the Rose of Sharon, the Only One who has conquered death and the One who has dominion over death. He is the Son of God, the God who is so big and unimaginable for the whole heaven is His throne and the whole earth is His footstool

I think you should rejoice not just for being a prince but that your name is in God's Book of life. Rejoice that Jesus Christ found and chose you; rejoice, you are His *bièn aimé!*

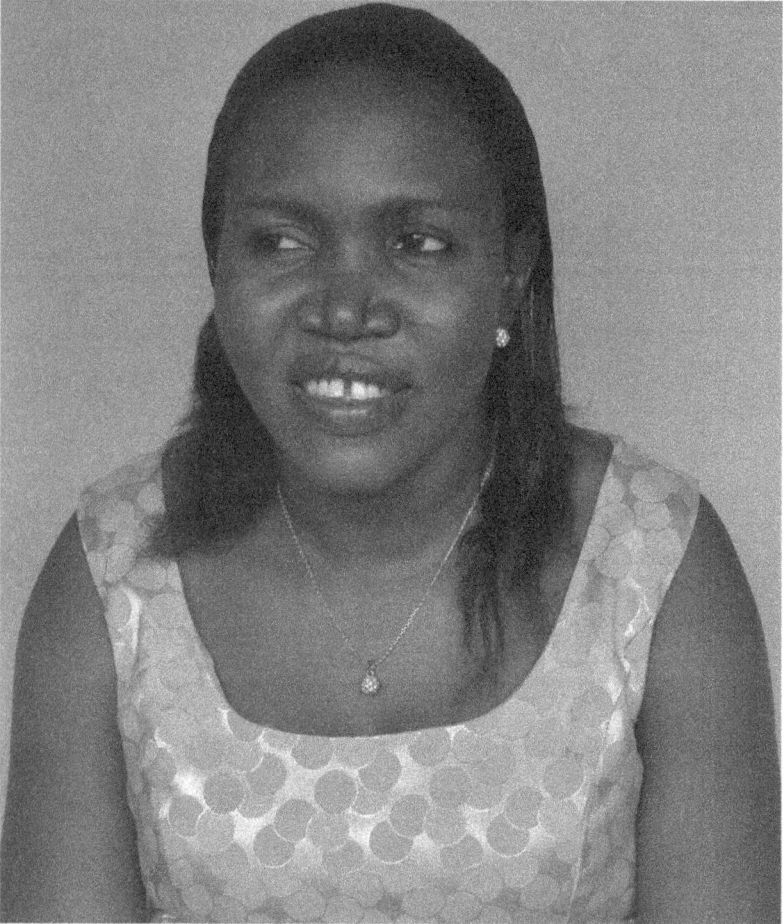

"One day of Glory and Excellence is far better than a million years of mediocrity." - Agu Jaachynma N.E.

Chapter Nine

Great Family Re-Union

One major criterion required in family re-union is your strong faith in God! The strength and length of your challenges or oppositions don't count, what counts is your faith. Your faith in God is what bridges the distance between you and your victory song!

The Bible says in **Hebrews 11:6,** *"But without faith it is impossible to please God, for he who comes to Him must believe that He is and that He is a Rewarder of those who diligently seek Him."*

The testimony of Jabez in the Bible is quite inspirational. The guy was named *"sorrow"*; he had everything working against him. He could have chosen to live and die in shame but he preferred fame, he could have chosen to remain a mediocre but he preferred honour! He wanted to stand out against all odds.

I am sure he was inspired by scriptures like: **Jeremiah 33:3,** *"Call upon me, and I will answer you, and show you great and mighty things which you do not know."*

Hebrews 13: 5 *"...I will never leave you nor forsake you."*

1st Peter 2:9, *"But you are a chosen generation, a royal priesthood, a holy nation, His own special people, that you may* *proclaim the praises of Him who called you out of darkness into His marvellous light."*

1ˢᵗ Peter 5:7, *"Casting all your care upon Him for He cares for you."*

Isaiah 54:4, *"Do not fear for you will not be ashamed; nor be disgraced, for you will not be put to shame; for you will forget the shame of your youth, and will not remember the reproach of your widowhood anymore"*

Having studied all these he therefore went to God in prayer with an amazing faith. He prayed to God with confidence and great faith. Read his prayer in (**1ˢᵗ Chronicles 4:10**): *"Oh, that you would bless me indeed, and enlarge my territory, that your hand would be with me, and that you would keep me from evil, that I not cause pain!" So God granted him what he requested!*

He didn't go to God whimpering, trembling, sniffing and twisting his hands behind his back. Neither did he go to Him stammering and standing on one leg while making webs with his fingers. He approached God with confidence and I tell you God loves such guys!

Notice that Jabez never went back after his prayers to living an accursed life or still needing sympathy from people. He got up and began to reign. After his prayers he knew God has heard him and answered him. His countenance was no more sad.

Anyone who is a part of this great family re-union must be a God seeker. You can't be a member of a family you know little or nothing about. **2nd Chronicles 15:2** says: *"The Lord is with you while you are with Him. If you seek Him, He will be found by you; but if you forsake Him, He will forsake you".*

Even in our biological families, we have family ethics and values. The prodigal son on returning home got back to doing things according to the family norms. The era of waking up in the morning and partying with prostitutes and alcoholics was gone. He was back home where there were set rules and principles. It is the same in our heavenly home, in God's family where the pauper-turned-Prince now belongs, there are certain ways you are expected to behave, certain things you are expected to do.

One of such important principles is :

Taking God's words very seriously... *"All scripture is given by inspiration of God, and is profitable for doctrine, for reproof, for correction, for instruction in righteousness that the man of God may be complete, thoroughly equipped for every good work"* **(2nd Timothy 3:16 & 17)**

"Your WORDS were found and I ate them, and your WORD

was to me the joy and rejoicing of my heart; for I am called by your name, O Lord God of hosts!" **(Jeremiah 15:16)**

Your reaction to God's words, your attitude to the things of the Spirit will go a long way to show if you are among those called together for this great family reunion.

2) **Learn to hear God**… **John 8:47** says, *"He that is of God heareth God's words; ye, therefore, hear them not, because ye are not of God."*

Brother, God speaks! Do you hear Him when He speaks to you? Jesus said in **John 10:27**, *"My sheep hear my voice, and I know them, and they follow me."*

As you leave the *"Pauperic"* state, adorned with the princely garments and accessories; then you should hear your Father's voice when He talks to you. You should pay heed to His instructions as well. Some people will say *"as I was praying, "something" said to me"* No! By all means No! God is not *"something"* God is your Father, the compassionate Father! He knows all you are going through, He feels what you feel. He longs for your company, He wants your love and attention always!

The love overtures of God to the love of His life (*you*) can be seen clearly in the Books of **Hosea** and in

Songs of Solomon. For space and time let's look at that of Hosea alone.

"Therefore, behold, I will allure her, and bring her into the wilderness, and speak comfortably unto her. I will give her, her vineyards from thence, and the valley of Achor as a door of hope; she shall sing there, as in the days of her youth, as in the day when she came up from the land of Egypt.

And it shall be, in that day, says the Lord that you will call me, My Husband, and no longer my Master, for I will take from her mouth the names of Baals, and they shall be remembered by their name no more. In that day I will make a covenant for them with the beasts of the field, with the birds of the air, and with the creeping things of the ground. Bow and sword of battle I will shatter from the earth, to make them lie down safely.

I will betroth you to me forever, yes, I will betroth you to me, in righteousness and justice, in loving kindness and mercy; I will betroth you to me in faithfulness, and you shall know the Lord. It shall come to pass in that day that I will answer, says the Lord; I will answer the heavens and they shall answer the earth. The earth shall answer with grain, with new wine, and with oil; they shall answer Jezreel. Then I will sow her for myself in the earth, and I will have mercy on her who had not obtained mercy; then I will say to those who were not my people, you are my people! And they shall say, you are my God!" (Hosea 2:14-23)

The Lord desires a beautiful relationship with all His

children; He is a loving Father who always wants the best for all His children. God wants you as a member of His family to delight yourself in Him and He will give you all of your heart's desires!

3). **Learn to access and utilize the blessings released to you**...God doesn't like waste so what do you do with the extra? You should distribute them. God is committed to giving you your daily bread **Psalm 23: 1(AMP)** *says "The Lord is my Shepherd {to feed, guide, and shield me}, I shall not lack".*

When He has made available to you all that you require and you have plenty, remember to give back to Him as well as give others too. After Jesus fed the five thousand and four thousand people respectively, He told His disciples to pick up the leftover not because He wanted to know the quantity but because He doesn't like waste, He wanted it to be properly accounted for.

Will it be right for the prodigal son to remain wasteful after he got home? Will Jacob and his family that have been in severe want and lack in his country come over to Egypt to waste resources? It won't be ideal; in fact, people around will term them ingrates. God doesn't want us to be called names hence His instruction to us that we distribute our surplus to those who lack.

Romans 12:13 says: *"Distributing to the needs of the saints, given to hospitality."*

Apostle Paul wrote in his admonition to Timothy, his son in the Lord…*"Command those who are rich in this present age not to be haughty, nor to trust in uncertain riches but in the living God, who gives us richly all things to enjoy. Let them do good, that they be rich in good works, ready to give, willing to share, storing up for themselves a good foundation for the time to come, that they may lay hold on eternal life"* (1st Timothy 6:17-19)

As one who has been re-united with Christ, who is now a member of God's family, you should not ride high through another's downfall rather aid grace in another person's life and speed up more works of grace for yourself. Remember a candle loses nothing by lighting another candle. You sure do not deserve all that you have been given so don't be a stumbling block or a hindrance to others.Don't blow off another's candle for it won't make yours shine brighter.

As a re-united member of God's family allow brotherly love to continue. Be content with such things as you have and wait patiently for God to lift you higher. Remember! Your dreams don't make you; you make your dreams!

"Praising Him raises you, it gives you a defence and delivers His manifested Presence to you."
~Agu, Jaachynma N.E.

Chapter Ten

Are You Involved?

W*elcome* to the last chapter of this great book. It's not a coincidence that the opening chapter of this book started with a question and the closing chapter equally started with a question. There are no coincidences in God's programme, all things are divinely arranged.

The theme of this chapter can be interpreted in several ways – are you involved? Are you part of those paupers who are now princes? Are you involved in an intimate relationship with God the Father, son and Holy Spirit? Are you among those whose *"Pauperic"* situations have been exchanged at the Cross of Calvary? In essence, do you accept that your debts have been paid and forgiven? Has your infirmities been taken, has your grief, pains and sicknesses being borne? Have you been redeemed from the curse of the Law? Have you returned home with the Prince? Are you part of the great family re-union gathering? If your answer to all these questions is "YES" then accept my hearty congratulations and let me re-echo the Words of our Lord and saviour Jesus Christ to you *"Come, you blessed of my father, inherit the Kingdom prepared for you from the foundation of the World"*

But if your answer to the above questions is *"No"* or you are not too sure, I will oblige you to go back to chapter three of this book and pray the sinner's prayer written there. Your life will become meaningful if you do that with all your heart. Don't heed to the whisperings of the enemy, he has nothing good and useful to offer you, he is only looking for people that will be tormented in hell fire with him.

That is not your lot. Hell-fire is made for Satan and his angels. I am sure you are not one of his angels, if you are you wouldn't be reading this book. It is important you get involved in God's kingdom principles, it is imperative you become a member of this great family. Talk to God about your state and He will change your heart and deliver your estates to you.

And for those of us already involved, here a few principles to keep us focused and on course...

Learn to talk like God. Don't talk fear; talk   faith. The whole world was created by words - word of faith. You can recreate your world with God's word in your mouth! Remember faith and fear originates from the same source – Words!

One of my favourite scriptures is **Mark 11:23**... *"for assuredly, I say to you, whoever says to this mountain, be thou removed and be cast into the sea and does not doubt in his heart, but believes that those things he says will come to pass, he will have whatever he says"*

Notice that Jesus didn't say *"whosoever shall cry unto this mountain, or complain about this mountain or even speak to God about this mountain"* He said to speak directly to the mountain! It may sound quite unconvincing and foolish but remember, *"God uses the foolish things of this world to confound the wise"* **1ˢᵗ Corinthians 1:27**.

If you want to continually put the enemy where he belongs right under your feet then you better keep talking like God! *"God calleth those things that be not as though they were"* **Romans 4:17**.

Did you see that? God called the non-existent things, talked about them as though they are already in existence that sure is faith!

Remember, expressing your faith in words is talking like God. We don't talk to posses them; we talk because we already have them.

You might now ask, *"what if nothing happens right away? What if the mountain still remains? What if the job didn't come"*? Remember; when Jesus cursed the fig tree in the Bible, nothing happened right away. The leaves of the tree were still green but Jesus was not moved, the important thing is that the word has gone forth! Don't bother about the *"what ifs"*, once you speak, consider it done and it will be done. Remember, we don't say it because we want to see it, we say it because it is so! The fig tree was discovered dead the next day, your own next day may be a week, a month, several months or even years for a thousand years in our sight are like an evening gone in God's sight. When the clouds are full of rain, they empty themselves on the earth. Your cloud must be full before the rains will come, so keep talking. Again, the speed of the process depends on your knowledge of God's principles and its applications. The major principle is your faith; Pastor Chris Oyakhilome said " *faith always works, if it didn't work, then it wasn't faith.*"

Also, there are different kinds of plants, some bear fruits within weeks, some months, others years. The same is applicable to the Spiritual things, *"Be ye not sluggish but be among those who through faith and patience inherit the promises" (Hebrews 6:12).*

Always agree with God's words and allow your faith to speak. Don't talk the negative; build up your faith with your words. Always ask yourself *"Do I want what I just said to come to pass?"* If the answer is No, then stop and put yourself right. It's neither by might nor by power. You can do it if you genuinely pray the prayer the Psalmist prayed in **Psalms 141:3 (MSG)** *"Post a guard at my mouth, GOD, set a watch at the door of my lips."*

Always talk like God and according to His word not like the people of the world!

Remember it is grace that got you involved; it is grace that made you part of God's family, that same grace is still available to you.

Don't panic even in the midst of trials, have a right attitude towards trials for **2nd Corinthians 4:17-18** says: *"For our light affliction, which is but for a moment, is working for us a far more exceeding and eternal weight of Glory, while we do not look at the things which are seen, but at the things which are not seen. For the things which are seen are temporary, but the things which are not seen are eternal."*

Whatever you are going through now in form of trials and afflictions are mere shadows for Christ has taken care of the substances. Always be joyful even in affliction knowing that God will not abandon you there. He is Our Ever-present help in time of need, He is Our Strong Tower, we run into Him and we are safe and secured!

Trust God wholly. God is able to handle all that concerns you! *"Commit your works unto the Lord, and thy thoughts shall be established"* **(Proverbs 16:3).** He will adjust your thoughts, prune them and cause them to be like His. He will lead you to that level where you will always know what to do.

Being part of this end- time army and a member of this unique family entail your knowing God and His words. You are expected to give undivided attention to His words. Cherish His presence, learn His methods and build your confidence in Him by believing His words!

Everyone involved in this family must be a *worshipper*! You won't expect to be raised if you don't praise Him. When you praise Him, He gives you divine direction, He causes you to enjoy His presence. As you praise Him, He gives you His defence and becomes a wall of fire round about you. When you praise Him, you are sure of His divine protection.

Don't take the grace He outpoured on you for granted. It is grace that delivered salvation and its total package to you.

This grace is centred on Christ Jesus. The Bible says concerning Him in **John 1:16-17** *"And of His fullness we have all received and grace for grace. For the law was given through Moses, BUT GRACE and truth came through Jesus Christ."*

Grace and truth came through Jesus Christ. Without Christ there is no Grace. Grace teaches us how to live. As members of this great family, we are not to live our lives by chance rather by choice. We are not to live with ungodliness and worldly lusts rather we are to live soberly (*carefully*), righteously (*be in right standing with God*) and godly (*having faith like God and doing things like God!*).

Apostle Paul in his letter to Titus his son in the Lord says: *"For the grace of God that brings salvation has appeared to all men, teaching us that, denying ungodliness and worldly lusts, we should live soberly, righteously and godly in the present age."* **(Titus 2:11-12)**

Put the grace given to you to work and be active for the Gospel. There is no room for idleness in God's family! Look at the curriculum vitae of Jesus Christ, Our Perfect Example!

- He is a teacher (*Matthew 5:2*)

- He is a Healer (*Matthew 15:30*)

- He fulfilled the law (*Matthew 5:18*)

- He is Compassionate (*Matthew 20:34*)

- He is the Door (*John 10:9*)

- He is the Good Shepherd (*John 10:11*)

- He is the Resurrection and Life (*John 11:25*)

- He was a Servant to His disciples (*John 13:1*-8)

- He is the Way, the Truth and the Life (*John 14:6*)

- He is the True Vine (*John 15:1*)

- He prayed without ceasing (*John 17*)

- He is a Preacher (*Mark 1:38*)

- He is the Lord of the Sabbath (*Mark 2:28*)

- He is always thankful (*Mark 8:6*)

- He dislikes evil and filthiness (*Mark 11:15-19*)

- He dislikes sectarianism (*Luke 9:49-50*)

- He is the Saviour (*Luke 9:55-56*)

- He is a *Praiser* and always joyful (*Luke 10:21-22*)

- He is a Miracle Worker (*Luke 8:24-25*)

- He is the Christ of God (*Luke 9:18-19*)

Space and time will not allow us to continue but you have seen that He was not idle.

I often tell people, He is the Greatest Giver! Look at this poem...

He Is The Giver....

He gave the hungry bread to eat.

He gave the widow of Nain joy by restoring her son to life

He gave the lepers attention and cleansed them

He fed the spiritually hungry with God's word

He gave the disciples wisdom, knowledge and power

He gave the criminal on the cross pardon

He gave the Pharisees and Scribes something to think about

He gave the devil some Name to fear and worry about

He gave God the honour and glory due Him

He gave you pardon

He gave you freedom

He gave you life in abundance

You will have more

If you do one thing…

Give Him your life,

He is the Lord of your life

He is the Lord your God!

© *Jaachinma Iheanacho*

Christ's death and resurrection brought us salvation in its totality. He died and was raised for man's justification. With His resurrection, man now has dominion over sin and the ability to live for God. Are you still involved?

In this family, there is always reward for obedience and faithfulness. The story of Ruth - the Moabite and Naomi's daughter in law comes to mind here.

God spoke concerning her people – the Moabites that they are the enemies of the Israelites yet her faithfulness and love for God's people enlisted her amongst the genealogy of our Lord Jesus Christ.

Deuteronomy 23:3 says *"An Ammonite or Moabite shall not enter into the congregation of the LORD; even to their tenth generation shall they not enter into the congregation of the LORD for ever":* However, Ruth broke this jinx with her love and steadfastness to Naomi her Israelite mother-inlaw. Look at this …*"And Salmon begat Booz of Rachab; and Booz begat Obed of Ruth; and Obed begat Jesse"* **(Matthew 1:5).**

In the same vein, Rehab was justified by God and her household rescued irrespective of her trade and past life style. For seeking the good and preservation of the Israelite spies, she favoured God's righteous course and she didn't loose her reward. **Joshua 6:25** *"And Joshua saved Rahab the harlot alive, and her father's household, and all that she had; and she dwelleth in Israel even unto this day; because she hid the messengers, which Joshua sent to spy out Jericho"*

Love is the watchword in this family of God. Love is a strong feeling of deep affection for someone or something. Love is described as the fulfilment of all laws.

If you love someone, you will do him no wrong. The

entire chapter of **1ˢᵗ Corinthians 13** talks about love, verses **4 -8** of it says, *"Love never gives up, Love cares more for others than for self. Love doesn't want what it doesn't have. Love doesn't strut, doesn't have a swelled head. Love doesn't force itself on others, isn't always "me first", doesn't fly off the handle, doesn't keep score of the sins of others. Love doesn't revel when others grovel, takes pleasure in the flowering of truth, puts up with anything, trusts God always. Always looks for the best, never looks back but keeps going to the end. Love never dies, inspired speech will be over some day; praying in tongues will end; understanding will reach its limit"* **(MSG)**

Jesus taught us how to love, He prayed for those who inflicted pain on Him, He loved His accusers! Love is the key needed to attain greater heights and achieve great dreams. A lover never loses!

1 Corinthians 2:9 says *"Eye has not seen, nor ear heard, nor have entered into the heart of man, the things which God prepared for those WHO LOVE HIM!"*

Those who love God have unlimited access to victories, wealth and the great life. Jesus described love as the greatest commandment.

1 Peter 4:8 (MSG) says *"Most of all, love each other as if your life depended on it. Love makes up for practically anything"*

If you say you are a member of this family and you are not

operating on the platform of love, you are a liar! God loved us and gave us His only begotten son! You can give without loving but you can't love without giving! You want to remain involved? Then LOVE!

When you walk in love, you walk in God's rest. There is rest for members of God's family; they operate under the umbrella of grace and favour. They know no lack and dwell in abundance of all good things always. The death and resurrection of Christ brought rest to everyone who accepts and acknowledges all that Christ did for humanity.

God rested on the seventh day after creating the whole world, He created man on the sixth day so man's first day on earth was God's rest day. Man was born into rest but when Adam deviated from God's plan, he lost the rest and strayed into toiling and turmoil. Jesus came to bring man back into the rest of God and the gospel made this possible. Anyone who hears the gospel and believes enters into God's rest and those who don't believe it enter into everlasting damnation.

Hebrews 4: 2-3: *"For indeed the gospel was preached to us as well as to them; but the word which they heard did not profit them, not being mixed with faith in those who heard it. For we who have believed do ENTER THAT REST, as He has said: "so I swore in my wrath, they shall not enter my rest", although the works were finished from the foundation of the world."*

When you let God into your life, He in turn lets you enter His rest. There are no struggles, panic, fear, worry et al in God's rest.

I encourage you to let go off every worry and let God, this is the only condition that qualifies you for His rest!

When the prodigal son came back to his father's house, he entered his father's domain of peace. He no longer bothered as to where the next meal will come from or who will take care of his other needs.

Joseph, after reuniting with his family felt comfortable and at peace with everyone and everything around him. He entered his rest and relaxed knowing he wouldn't have to worry again as to whether his father and brothers have been destroyed by the famine. He had them around him so he was at peace.

This is how it ought to be with every child of God who has returned home to God through Jesus Christ. There should no longer be cares and worries for we have entered into God's rest. This is why Jesus Christ calls out to us in the Book of **Matthew 11:28-30**: *"Come to me, all you who labour and are heavy laden and I will give you REST. Take my yoke upon you and learn from me, for I am gentle and lowly in heart and you will find REST for your souls. For my yoke is easy and my burden is light!"*

In Christ, there is peace, in the world there are pains and tribulation but following the path God earmarked for us through Jesus Christ guarantees our safety and rest. Little wonder the Psalmist said in **Psalm 16:11** *"You will show me the path of life; in your presence is fullness of joy; at your right hand are pleasures forever more"*

There is fulfilment, upliftment, grace, blessings and rest for genuine members of God's family. When you enter His rest, you cease from fighting your own battles and start enjoying His own victories!

Conclusion

In conclusion, Christ is on our side, none can effectively be against us. Christ called us princes none can call us paupers. We are Joint-Heirs with Jesus Christ nobody can call us outcasts.

 We are children of God. We have been raised to a height that is unattainable and unimaginable for the natural man. We have won battles that are strange and strong for a carnal man to win.

Our paths are therefore shinning brighter and brighter and will do so until the perfect day because we are God's righteousness in Christ.

What should we say for such great work of salvation that Christ wrought for us? What should we tell God for sending His Only begotten Son to die in our stead? This act reconciled us to God and committed to us the ministry of reconciliation. All we have to say is just Thank You Lord!

Thanksgiving gladdens God's heart. When you are grateful for what He's done for you, He lifts you to a higher altitude. When you don't appreciate, you depreciate. Gratitude is an attitude that takes you to a higher altitude with multitude of the beatitude!

The Pauper is welcomed home at last. His soul has found rest; he has tasted both sides of life and has drawn his conclusion and learnt so many life's lessons. With these lessons, his life has become a testimony and a manual for teaching others.

One of the teachings the Pauper came up with is assigning a new meaning to each letter of the English Alphabets in the following order.

A – **A**bove all trials and pains.

B – **B**eyond the tears and hurts.

C – **C**ries of agony and frustration.

D – **D**well in praise path and park

E – **E**very challenge has an expiry date.

F – **F**rustrations don`t last forever.

G – **G**od`s grace is everly sufficient.

H – **H**ope with patience is mostly effective.

I – **I**gnorance robs one of his blessings.

J – Joining yourself to God`s ability is the best.

K – Keep your praise high and flying always.

L – Let God`s Word dwell in you richly.

M – Make His service your delight

N – Never give up on your faith.

O – On Christ the Solid Rock stand.

P – Pressing towards the mark of your calling.

Q – Questions of life are answered in Him.

R – Rest is guaranteed in His presence.

S – Stand tall against all odds.

T – Trust His plans and purposes for you.

U – Unleash your faith and get the best of life.

V – Victory is your birthright, you know.

W – Worship delivers the victories to you.

X – `Xcellence and Greatness are His plans for you.

Y – You will have them if you believe and

Z – Zealously remain in Zion

The pauper has reached his peak, he has arrived Zion even while still alive. He has grasped the promises of God and has endorsed all. The Pauper now declares, "*I am too blessed to be stressed!*" He has realized truly that the shortest distance between a problem and a solution is the distance between his knees and the floor. He says "the *one who kneels to the Lord can truly stand up to anything*" You can do it. Your story can be changed, your future can be sutured, and your dreams can be realized in the presence of your Maker. Lay those troubles at His feet today and be free forever more! **Learn to Give Thanks!**

A Christian that is not thankful will remain at the low ebbs of life. I will stress here that Gratitude is an altitude that takes you to an altitude with multitude of beatitude.

Our prayer meetings shouldn't be more important than our thanksgiving services for a thankful heart is a delight to the Lord!

Bibliography

(1) Faith food Devotions by Kenneth E. Hagin

(2) God at work today (*Publication of Living Faith Church, Abuja*)

(3) King James Version of the Bible

(4) New King James Version of the Bible

(5) None of these Diseases By Pastor Chris Oyakhilome

(6) Rhapsody of Realities Daily Devotional By Re, (Dr.) Chris Oyakhilome. Ph.D

Be a Prince: Answer Your God-Given Name...Take Those Limitations Off Your Life and Rule Your World.

ABOUT THE AUTHOR

Agu Jaachynma N.E. is a successful, dynamic, prolific and Best-Selling Author. A Graduate of Languages and Linguistics Department of the Prestigious University of Jos, Nigeria; a Principal Administrative Officer with the Federal Government Establishment, a loving wife, a caring mother, a teacher, a mentor and an advocate of women empowerment.

She is the Executive Director of the KingsTreasureHouse Concept; a highly respected role model and an inspiration to many. She shares motivational insight with folks in her generation and those yet to be born via her write-ups, books et al. She lives in Nigeria with her beloved family comprising of her heartthrob: Dr. Aham and their two Gorgeous Heritages from the Lord: KING and EDWALD.

www.ingramcontent.com/pod-product-compliance
Lightning Source LLC
LaVergne TN
LVHW041320080426
835513LV00008B/522